MAKE YOURSELF *Memorable*

WINNING STRATEGIES TO HELP YOU
MAKE A GREAT IMPRESSION ON YOUR
BOSS, YOUR CO-WORKERS, YOUR
CUSTOMERS — AND EVERYONE ELSE!

STEPHANIE G. SHERMAN
with V. CLAYTON SHERMAN

D0711548

amacom
American Management Association
New York • Atlanta • Boston • Chicago • Kansas City • San Francisco • Washington, D.C.
Brussels • Mexico City • Tokyo • Toronto

This book is available at a special
discount when ordered in bulk quantities.
For information, contact Special Sales Department,
AMACOM, a division of American Management Association,
135 West 50th Street, New York, NY 10020.

Library of Congress Cataloging-in-Publication Data

Sherman, Stephanie G.
  *Make yourself memorable: winning strategies to help you make a great
  impression on your boss, your co-workers, your customers—and everyone else! /
  Stephanie G. Sherman with V. Clayton Sherman.*
      p. cm.
  Includes bibliographical references and index.
  ISBN 0-8144-7913-8
  *1. Career development.   2. Self-presentation.   3. Success in business.
  I. Sherman, V. Clayton.   II. Title*
HF5381.S543 1996
650.1—dc20   *96-3981*
                                                                CIP

Printing number
10   9   8   7   6   5   4   3   2   1

To my **mother** and **father**, who have made themselves
memorable to me in so many ways.

To my children, **Jonathan** and **Adam**, who continually remind
me of what is important in life.

Most of all to my **husband**, whose never-ending support,
charitable ear, down-to-earth advice, and painstaking editorial
suggestions have made this book a reality.

Contents

Who Should Read This Book?

This book is for any persons—or organizations—who want to enhance their relationships with others and create a personally memorable image. You with your customers or boss, colleagues, friends, spouse, or other family members.

If you are in a competitive situation in either your professional or personal life and are looking for strategies to advance, or defend, your present position, this book is for you. If you are in a personal or professional relationship that is stagnating or declining, and you want to rejuvenate that relationship, this book is for you. Or, if you simply want to create a new, more memorable and lasting relationship with someone, for whatever reason, this book is for you.

Relationships are the best part of life. However, most people do not realize that their relationships and personal image can be immensely enhanced with the assistance of a few changes in basic behavior. In fact, many people do not realize that it is their image, or lack thereof, not who they are as a person, that is contributing to a declining relationship or a stagnating career. Borrowing from the idea of a makeover, like those we have seen in beauty advertisements and home improvement guides, the potential for being a memorable person already resides within each person. We believe in you, but you may need to be renewed or revitalized. Without a prescription or recipe, people do not know how to conduct a personal renewal. With this book as a guide, anyone can quickly make modifications that will bring them lasting success in their relationships.

How the Book Is Organized

The book is organized in four parts. Part One and Chapter 1 describe the basic formula for a winning image. Each formula factor is supported with specific examples, checklists, do's and don'ts. The basic formula can be used with all audiences and quickly creates a positive, memorable initial impact, or converts past unfavorable impressions into positive images.

Part Two, comprised of Chapters 2 through 6, is dedicated to a detailed examination of each of the five strategies that can be used to create a memorable image.

Chapter 2 addresses innovation as a memory-making strategy. How to create the types of innovation that become memorable, sources of innovative ideas, and ways to preserve the memorable status of your innovative efforts are discussed.

Chapter 3 explores the immense value and applications of imagination as a memory-making strategy, and how to unleash the powers of this underutilized quality to create a memorable status.

Chapter 4 focuses on a global application of the concept of presentation, which is defined as a way of being and doing things, including the presentation of messages, ideas, gifts, events, and self. Whether it is in a personal or professional, public or private setting, the prescription for all presentations promises to create a memorable event.

Chapter 5 introduces the "M factors," or memorable boosters, and describes how to create and use these to make yourself memorable.

Chapter 6 describes how to create and use unexpected incidents to make yourself memorable, and how to transform routine events into memorable ones.

Used singularly, or in combination, each strategy has a different potential impact depending on the type of audience being addressed. Characteristics, techniques, and the how to and when to directives are included in each chapter, making each chapter self-sufficient.

Part Three, being Chapter 7, is dedicated to the artistic application and pragmatic techniques of influential persuasion. Conversations, discussions, negotiations, and direct persuasive appeals comprise a large portion of relationships. The facts and artistic application governing persuasive efforts and projected outcomes are imperative to creating a memorable and successful image and presentation. In a concise, ready-to-use fashion, the do's and the don'ts, the positioning of persuasive arguments, and the strategies for successful persuasion are presented.

Part Four, comprised of Chapters 8 through 11, is organized around the type of audience you wish to make yourself memorable to. It is full of lists of actions you can take and ideas you can use to boost your memorable image with any audience.

Chapter 8, "Make Yourself Memorable to Customers," offers strategies, behaviors, and prescriptions to follow to entice people to become your customer and to remain your customer. The prescriptions here will cause you to leap ahead of the competition and become the "vendor of choice."

Chapter 9, "Make Yourself Memorable to Your Boss," addresses the idea of getting ahead by getting noticed and becoming indispensable in this throwaway world. This chapter provides strategies to make you the most memorable and critically needed person in the opinion of your boss, colleagues, work mates, or other select decision-making groups.

Chapter 10, "Make Yourself Memorable to Family and Friends," explains which behaviors and attitudes, if appropriately applied, can change dutiful moms and dads into memorable, magic-making moms and dads. And how to build love, honesty, dependability, generosity, and family identity into your family relationships.

Chapter 11, "Consolation Prizes," addresses the probability of making yourself memorable in any given relationship or situation, and sets forth a list of readiness factors that suggest when there is a high probability of making yourself memorable, assuming that the prescribed behaviors are carried out. It also sets forth a list of no-win readiness factors, elements that suggest a less than desirable result regardless of the amount and type of resources you have dedicated to the effort of making yourself memorable.

Can you make yourself memorable and rise above the crowd? Yes! Now is the time to take hold of your image and sculpt it into what your inner heart and mind want you to be. With some discipline and conscientious effort, you will become memorable, and the important relationships of your life will become enriched. Let the real you come through for the fun of it and the achievement of those things you most desire.

Acknowledgments

Although only the authors' names appear on the cover of *Make Yourself Memorable*, many people have generously contributed their time and ideas to making this book a reality. We are indebted to them. A special thanks to those friends, colleagues, and family members who have provided support and/or insightful concepts and comments that have contributed to the creation of the final product. And a special acknowledgment of the work of the many writers, theorists, editors, and researchers who are credited in the bibliography.

A special professional thanks to Mary Glenn, Acquisitions Editor at AMACOM Books, for her enthusiasm and her support of these ideas even before the final manuscript was in place, and to the AMACOM staff for their insightful editorial comments and direction.

The quotations you'll see at the beginnings of the parts and chapters of this book, as well as some that appear in the text, were taken from *The Forbes Scrapbook of Thoughts on the Business of Life* (New York: B.C. Forbes & Sons Publishing Co., Inc., 1976); *The Forbes Scrapbook of Thoughts on the Business of Life II* (New York: B.C. Forbes & Sons Publishing Co., Inc., 1984); Louis E. Boone, *Quotable Business* (New York: Random House, 1992); William Safire and Leonard Safire, *Good Advice* (Avenel, N.J.: Wing Books, 1992); and Richard Evans, *Richard Evans' Quote Book* (Salt Lake City: Publishers Press, 1971).

Part One

Make Yourself Memorable

"You can have anything you want if you want it desperately enough. You must want it with an inner exuberance that erupts through the skin and joins the energy that created the world."

— Sheilah Graham

Think of the most memorable people you have known in your personal life, your career, and all your business experiences. What do they all have in common that made them memorable to you? If you can't identify the common links between these memorable people, don't worry. Keep these people in mind as you read the principles and applications given in this book. By the time you have finished, you will be able to identify how and why each of these people made themselves memorable to you.

Ever wonder why a co-worker is selected for promotion while you're passed over? Or why one colleague gains more attention than others? Why is it that some people break through and land challenging and rewarding assignments while others make far less progress? Or why some people seem to have rewarding, memorable relationships, while others struggle to try and create a relationship worth having. The answer to these questions, and thus the secret to boosting your image, career, and business, lies in your ability to package and present yourself in a memorable way.

To be memorable could mean the difference between a career promotion or finding yourself in the plateau trap. Between personal success or mediocrity. Between celebrity or unappreciated labor. And between merely feeling good or feeling great about yourself.

Interestingly enough, there is no one special talent, skill, or characteristic that makes one person more memorable than another. It does not require a special God-given talent or beauty. Rather, it is the "package" of characteristics, or personal image, that an individual has that is appealing to others, and consequently memorable. Thus, all people have the capacity to make themselves memorable—to rocket to higher levels of career achievement, develop more meaningful relationships, and achieve their personal desires—if they are willing to do the work described in this book.

Winning Professional Images: The Basic Formula

The formula for making yourself memorable is amazingly simple (see Figure P-1).

Three primary factors—style, substance, and timing—influence how others perceive you and what you represent. The challenge is to simultaneously balance all three factors while maximizing each opportunity to make yourself memorable.

As with mathematical formulas, laws of nature, and cookbook recipes, each element of the formula—style, substance, and timing—plays an important role in helping you to reach the desired result. Each element must simultaneously be in place for the full magic of the formula to work. The absence of one element cancels out the positive effects of the balance of the formula. Weakness in one element dilutes the desired results. For example, a person of great style may initially be invited to the executive suite, but will quickly be ushered to the exit door as weakness in substance becomes apparent. Or, in another situation, the components of style and substance may be strong, but the element of timing is unmanageable; thus the message and the messenger become lost in a sea of other priorities.

The reverse is also true. The stronger each element of the formula is, the stronger the resulting personal image will be. When style, substance, and timing are equally strong, there is a substantial probability that you and your message will become memorable—and reap all the rewards that come with memorability.

Figure P-1   Memorability formula.

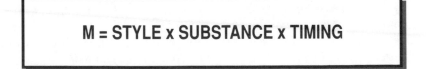

M = STYLE x SUBSTANCE x TIMING

1

The Winning Formula

"Pick me, pick me, oh please, pick me!"
—America's playgrounds

Memorability Formula = *Style* × Substance × Timing

Style is the manner in which one presents oneself. There are four interlocking elements of style; when brought together successfully, these four elements create an attractive, winning style, or manner of self-presentation (see Figure 1-1).

Each of the formula elements is simple. However, as with an algebraic formula, the absence or weakness of one element of the formula is damaging to the total image. But when all elements are in place, a highly desirable and memorable image is created—one that draws others to you like a magnet, making you memorable.

Let's explore the elements of style by studying the common characteristics of those who are memorable. Make a list of action items for your individual style development plan.

Figure 1-1   The four elements of style.

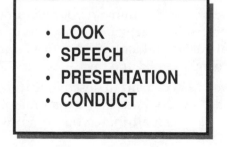

- **LOOK**
- **SPEECH**
- **PRESENTATION**
- **CONDUCT**

Fitting Your Style to Success

To achieve success, create a look of success. Use the basic "as if" technique. The technique suggests that if you want to possess a quality, such as the quality of success, then you should act "as if" you already have that quality. If your goal is to become an executive, then create a look for yourself that is like that of those occupying the executive suite. Observe the behavior and the appearance of your boss, your boss's boss, and the company president. Duplicate the image they project, and consistently look and behave in a likable and impeccable manner. *Fit your style to your desired position in life.*

If you sift through the images of hundreds of successful, high-profile people, you will consistently note certain common style elements for men and certain common style elements for women. Make a list of these elements and check your look of success against this list.

The Look of Success for Men

Use the following guide to direct your decision making in wardrobe selection and general outward appearance. It would not be unusual if your personal preferences initially differed from these recommendations. Adjust your preferences to your new image as reflected in the following conservative guidelines. The goal is to create a look of success and a style of being that does not distract from the substance you represent. Like the advice that Cary Grant's father gave, and it obviously worked, "Let them see you, and not the suit. That should be secondary."

Remember, it is not as important for each specific guideline to be adhered to as it is for the underlying principle to be followed.

1. *Stay basic.* Conventional navy blue and dark gray suits, slacks, and jackets should command your wardrobe. These colors are rich and universally acceptable, project an unmistakably serious professional image, and look good with all skin tones and hair colors. Leave other patterned and trendy suits to your competitors.

2. *Go natural.* Choose natural design lines for suits and shirts. Leave oversized shoulder pads and unnatural looks on the rack. They appear artificial, an attribute you do not want ascribed to

you. Artificiality connotes a falseness that can spill over onto your image. Choose natural fabrics, colors, and materials. This means cotton and wool, not polyester or man-made fabrics. Leather for shoes, belts, and accessories, not plastic or man-made fabrics. Choose white, beige, and other natural colors for shirts. Avoid bright and blended colors, checked or patterned designs.

3. *Keep it simple.* Limit the number and type of accessories and jewelry you wear. Belts should be of leather, with a small buckle, and match the shoe color and fabric. A wedding band and class ring are maximum accessories, and never worn on the same hand. Lapel pin, bracelet, earring, tie tacks, and tattoos are out. Socks should be a dark, solid color. Pockets are to be empty—no wallet, comb, pen and pencil set, key ring, or other bulky items. No plastic or rubber watch band, canvas or steel briefcase, or cartoon character necktie. Suspenders are preferred to belts, but never are the two worn together. Elegance is in the simplicity of the look. Uncluttered is what you want to be.

4. *Make it fit.* Choose clothes that fit. Beware of shirts that are small and gap across the chest, or have pilled or sagging colors, and of shirt sleeves that pull above the wrist. Invest in proper-fitting slacks. Avoid pants that are tight with gapping pockets, pulled zippers, and stretched seams. Keep body dimensions and curves your secret.

5. *Keep it covered.* Some things are better kept private. T-shirts should never show. Chest hair, leg hair, and arm hair are better kept secret. This means tall socks, long sleeves, and tight shirt collars. Sneaky tufts of hair at the collar, leg, or anywhere are unacceptable.

6. *Look clean and crisp.* Heavy starch for shirts and slacks yields a crisp, organized look. A professional haircut is a must. If baldness dominates, go natural. Toupees and wraparound hairstyles suggest artificiality, an unbecoming characteristic. Go easy on cologne. Light fragrances lightly applied are preferable to overwhelming ones. Watch for dandruff, stains on the shirt, tie, or socks, and dirt under the nails. See your dentist regularly for hygienic cleaning and repair. A smile is the door to your first conversation. Make it inviting.

7. *Be calm and controlled.* Control nervous habits. Sit still and back in the chair, legs crossed at the knee, if you must. Thumb

twiddling, gum chewing, doodling, finger tapping, leg rocking, mustache rolling, beard stroking, cigarette smoking, paper rolling, and head bobbing are all offputting.

8. *Stay fit.* A physically fit physique projects an image of high self-esteem, of someone who cares about themself. Not everyone can be perfectly fit physically, nor is that expected. However, a reasonable range of fitness is expected. Obesity or other physical extremes could be distracting and make you unfavorably memorable.

The Look of Success for Women

Guidelines for women are like those for men, although the application is different. There are many more commercial choices for a women's appearance. Don't get distracted from the basic guidelines provided, however. Fashion flair creativity is not a friend to the successful look.

1. *Keep it simple.* Clothing should be basic and simple. No plaids, stripes, florals, or checks. A loose-fitting jacket, blouse, or sweater with a dark-colored skirt is the preferred look. A conservative, professional appearance that does not sacrifice a sense of femininity is the goal. Dresses should employ a simple, basic design line. Avoid floral, add-ons, lace, and ruffles. People should notice you, not what you are wearing, which is contrary to what the fashion industry promotes. Clothes that scream, "Look at me!" are not for you.

2. *Keep it covered.* Avoid low necklines, cleavage, bare arms or shoulders, short skirts, long slits up the skirt or pant leg, hanging slips, bare legs, cut-out shoes, or see-through blouses.

3. *Think small.* When it comes to accessories, choose small earrings, sleek handbags, low heels, and clear eyeglasses. Limit jewelry to a wedding band and small watch. Matching belt, shoes, handbag, and briefcase make for a "together" look.

4. *Make it light and natural.* Fragrances and makeup should be barely perceptible—natural and light. Fluid and natural hairstyles are the most youthful and becoming. Lightly tanned skin tones or rosy cheeks suggest a healthy, vibrant person. A bright attractive smile breaks down barriers, inviting intelligent conversation.

5. *Stay calm and controlled.* Avoid nervous habits, including hair twirling, playing with earrings, leg rocking, pencil tapping, scratching, gum chewing, paper rolling, toe tapping, body rocking, cigarette smoking, or head bobbing.

Most retail stores promote trendy fashionable items, not necessarily those that fit your new smart, professional, and successful image. What's "in style" is very likely no longer the style for you. For basic wardrobe needs, shop at Brooks Brothers, Lands' End, Hart/Shaffner/Marx, and other traditional conservative clothiers. Most of these retailers also offer catalog shopping. Avoid inexpensive stores, where product quality does not carry the look of success.

The Foundations of Memorable Conduct

How we conduct ourselves does make a difference. Abrasive conduct causes a distance to develop between you and others. Ordinary conduct causes you to go unnoticed. Memorable conduct raises you above the crowd.

There are four qualities of memorable conduct, which, when blended together, create a gravitational force, drawing others to you. These qualities can set you apart, and above the crowd (see Figure 1-2).

Any one of the four attributes alone is admirable but insufficient to create a memorable image. Packaged together, these qualities guarantee success. Let's define each quality in daily terms.

Figure 1-2 The four qualities of memorable conduct.

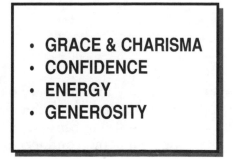

- **GRACE & CHARISMA**
- **CONFIDENCE**
- **ENERGY**
- **GENEROSITY**

Grace and Charisma

A combination of mannerly conduct and calmness of emotion is rare to find, yet easy to employ. Examples of charming, graceful behavior include such basics as:

- Holding doors open for others
- Assisting with garments and seating
- Serving others first
- Making a slight bow of the head to acknowledge another's presence
- Giving a kiss on the hand rather than the cheek
- Presenting elderly people first, then women and children
- Offering your seat to another
- Publicly recognizing your host/hostess with a toast
- Generously using "please," "thank you," "if you please," and "may I have the honor of…"
- Addressing audiences by personalizing them, for example, by saying "my dear friends," "my colleagues," or "my dear family"

Charismatic people display themselves as:

- Approachable and nonthreatening
- Having an interest in others
- Being respectful and confident in their actions and statements
- Being positively oriented toward people, places, and things
- Not taking themselves too seriously
- Compassionate, warm, caring, and empathetic toward others

Confidence

Step into the limelight. It's okay to call attention to yourself and to make your abilities known. Deborah Tannen, communications specialist and linguist, states in her best-selling book, *Talking From 9 to 5*, that judgment about confidence can be inferred only from the way people present themselves.* So, present yourself with confidence in order to be perceived as a confident person.

Build your confidence on the skills and achievements you have already proved. Display confidence in every manner of your being: your walk, your talk, and your attitude. Target areas for your confidence carefully and conservatively, ensuring that your level of confidence is not exaggerated, but is, in fact, an appropriate statement of your abilities. Take on unpopular or risker challenges in the areas where you are most confident of your abilities, and persevere until the challenge is fulfilled, all the while never compromising your personal values.

Demonstrate your leadership and confidence by reassuring the weak along the way and assisting the resource-poor. Stay the course. Don't let your confidence be shaken at any cost. No second-guessing about your decisions or actions. Go forward with the knowledge that you will succeed!

Characteristics of Confidence in Action

It is a more conservative and politically smart move to display and promote your confidence in areas where you have already demonstrated excellence. It is much riskier to exhibit confidence in an unproven area, where the level of confidence may be artificially high, thus causing an embarrassing situation for yourself if you are called upon to perform and cannot.

Test your competencies and adjust performance until it reaches a point at which you are confident that you can consistently perform at a high level. Then bring your confidence into the public arena.

To display an aura of confidence, sharpen your performance in the following two areas:

1. *The way you carry and conduct yourself.* Have excellent posture. No rounded shoulders, slouching stomachs, or dropped chins. Stand straight and tall. Carry yourself with an economy of

*Tannen, Deborah, *Talking From 9 to 5* (New York: William Morrow & Co., 1994), pp. 34–35.

movement, frequently called grace, moving to your destination without hesitancy, questions, or distraction.

2. *Your actions.* What you do as well as how you do it reflects your level of confidence. Highly confident people exhibit behavior that is:

- Reassuring
- Directive of others
- Without hesitancy
- Positioned in the leadership or up-front location
- Forward looking

For example, they initiate conversation, saying "hello" to people in elevators or when passing them in the hall, speak up in discussions, and move with a sense of purpose and direction.

Energy

I once heard that the difference between one man and another is not merely ability but energy. Energy is positive and contagious. It draws people to you, making you desirable to be with. Enthusiasm is a form of energy that attracts attention, invites conversation and discussion, and persuades easily.

A consistent display of enthusiasm and positive attitude saves time because there is never a need to explain why one is sad or bored. Regardless of your internal feelings, the external presentation must be consistently positive and enthusiastic in order to become memorable.

Four common characteristics of energized people are:

1. *They are always doing.* They are constantly engaged in some activity that is directed toward achieving their goal. They focus their activities in the direction of the goal and are protective of the time they have allotted for working toward that goal.

2. *They go full speed ahead.* The pace at which they operate is faster than normal. They work faster, talk faster, walk faster, do faster, going from one piece of work to the next with equal interest and speed. They are expert at time management and know how to put the least productive tasks toward the end of the day when personal energy and interest begin to fade.

3. *They are enthusiastic.* A positive, passionate interest dominates their attitude and activities. They refuse to hear the negatives of others or to dwell on the problems in situations. They view everything as an opportunity.

4. *They are constantly goal-directed.* Like a dog going for a bone, energized people never lose sight of the goal. They create visual representations and reminders of the goal and routinely track progress. They let nothing get in the way of their progress toward the goal.

Generosity

Generosity is the fourth quality of memorable conduct. It is that quality of personal giving that goes beyond what is needed or expected—and sometimes beyond what is reasonably capable of being given. Generous people give of themselves and their possessions frequently, with no expectation of a quid pro quo.

One might think that financial wealth is a prerequisite to generosity, but material status actually has nothing to do with the concept of generosity. Generosity is a state of mind dominated by self-giving at all levels. No-cost and low-cost giving are equally as powerful as substantial financial giving. The following ideas will get you started thinking in terms of daily generosity. Give them frequently.

Intangible Gifts

- Compliments
- Encouragement
- Time
- Special attention
- Appreciation
- Public recognition
- The benefit of learned wisdom
- The benefit of experience
- A personal opinion
- Music played for another
- Good wishes

Tangible Gifts

- A copy of your favorite poem or book
- A treasured keepsake
- Flowers from your garden
- Something to add to a collection
- A collection you have made
- Homemade baked goods
- Photo of a special event
- Ice cream
- A hug
- A kiss on the cheek
- Lyrics that convey a special sentiment

The Process of Giving Made Memorable

Many gifts are given that are not recognized for their real value. If you give the gift of time but don't label it a "gift of time," it is likely to be taken for granted as something else, something much less valuable. The same is true of material, tangible gifts. When you give a valued material possession but don't define it as such, it could be viewed as less than what it really is. For example, a one dollar bill given by a father to his son without further explanation remains simply a one dollar bill. However, if the story of this one dollar bill is told, the son would learn that it is the first dollar earned by his father, and as such represents the beginning of the family's financial future.

To give the wholeness of a gift in a memorable way, use the following three-step process:

1. *Tell.* Tell the recipient what you are going to give. Describe the item, where it came from, how you came to possess it, and why you want to give it to that person.
2. *Do.* Deliver the gift, using the principle of memorable presentation in Chapter 4 to boost the effectiveness of your delivery.
3. *Explain.* Tell the whole story of what you have given, why this gift is important to you, and what the recipient might want to do to retain the value of the gift.

Substance

Memorability Formula = Style × *Substance* × Timing

Although style is a prerequisite for gaining attention, it is the *substance* you represent that generates long-term interest in you. Style without substance is shallow—a one-time event. But style *with* substance, like sizzle with steak, is the winning combination to attract and retain personal attention and interest.

Substance is the content and message you represent. Messages are most memorable when they are:

1. *Factual.* Based on verifiable facts.

2. *Value-centered.* In support of one or more personal core values. These are the values by which you live your life, the values around which your character has developed—values such as respect, honesty, and personal dignity.

3. *Simple.* Concise, easily and quickly communicated.

4. *Emotionally linked.* Emotional links directly connect a concept, idea, or feeling to people by tapping into their emotional makeup of past or present feelings and experiences. An individual's emotional link personalizes and interprets the concept, idea, or feeling at a level that is easy for the person to understand and process. Individual emotional profiles vary greatly from person to person. Frequently accessed and memorably effective emotional links are:

- Caring
- Compassion
- Competition
- Love
- Pride
- Honor

Each of these emotional links has the ability to stand alone. However, the more elements you touch simultaneously, the more powerful the experience will be.

5. *Personalized.* Messages that are personalized contain elements and meaning that are unmistakably meant solely for a targeted person or audience.

6. *One-up.* One-up messages position you at a higher level than others, make you seem more credible, more expert, more

important. One way of separating yourself from others is to become more expert in an area than anyone else is. Become very close to expert subject information sources. Speak with all of them, not just a sampling. Be complete in your research. Visit with them personally. On-site research has more credibility and is therefore more powerful than remote research. While others report facts from secondary sources, you can report facts researched on "the site of..." or casually mention that "while I was visiting with..." you collected certain facts. This positions you "one up" from the others, giving you a more desirable and memorable status, a status that sets you apart from the crowd.

7. *Consistent.* What you represent and how you represent it must be in line with your personal values and the personal values of your audience. Let your guiding rule here be not how much you do but how well you do it. Choose things that express your own individuality, and look for quality rather than quantity.

Timing

Memorability Formula = Style × Substance × *Timing*

The third element in the formula to make yourself memorable is *timing.* When style and substance are strong but timing is unmanageable, then would-be memorable events are never born. Optimal timing, which translates into optimal receptivity, is an equally important factor in the overall formula for success. To identify optimal timing opportunities, or periods of greatest receptivity, refer to the Rule of Firsts.

Rule of Firsts

The Rule of Firsts is general in nature but widely applicable. It is based on the idea that personal energy, interest, and receptiveness are at their peak before any interruptions or distractions have occurred—and that interruptions and distractions are cumulative, wearing down personal energy, interest, and receptiveness as the day proceeds.

Following this principle of thought, the Rule of Firsts suggests that the best time slot, or most receptive period of time for a person, particularly your boss, is the first one.

- *First* day of the workweek.
- *First* part of the day.
- *First* meeting on the topic.
- *First* item on the agenda.

But because every individual has an idiosyncratic biological and psychological pattern of behavior, you may wish to confirm the Rule of Firsts by charting your boss's behavior.

To chart behavior, use a stack of 3 × 5 index cards, with each card representing a one-week period of time. Indicate the days of the week across the top of the card. Vertically, down the left side of the card, indicate one-hour time slots for the morning and the afternoon. Crosshatch the days and time of day for the week to create your chart, as in Figure 1-3.

Figure 1-3   Charting boss behavior.

	SUN	MON	TUE	WED	THU	FRI	SAT
8–9 AM							
9–10 AM							
10–11 AM							
11–12 AM							
12–1 PM							
1–2 PM							
2–3 PM							
3–4 PM							
4–5 PM							
Evening							

Now, test the hypothesis daily. As you encounter your boss at various times of day, and days of the week, rate his/her receptivity on a scale of one to ten. A rating of one indicates an outrageously bad mood, not receptive at all, and ten is an extremely positive and receptive mood. After several weeks of charting, a pattern will emerge. Note the highly receptive days and times of day as well as the highly resistant days and times of day.

The pattern you see may match the Rule of Firsts, or it may be different. Use your tested results to schedule yourself for optimal meeting and approachable times. Use the Rule of Firsts as a backup strategy. When optimal time slots are not available, schedule as close to the Rule of Firsts as possible, avoiding "deadly times."

Deadly Times to Avoid

Regardless of the greatness that your style and substance represent, success will not be yours if timing and receptivity are unmanaged. There are definite deadly time slots to avoid—periods of time when receptivity and interest levels, and therefore the probability of approval and support, are less than optimal. Often it is better to delay a meeting or presentation than it is to be slotted into one of the following death zones.

1. *Last on the agenda.* The last agenda item never receives the time or attention it deserves. People are pressured to conclude the meeting, anxious to leave, or just plain tired of sitting for a long time.

2. *Late afternoon meetings.* Late afternoon is the least productive time of the day. Friday afternoons are the worst of the worst. Minds wander to evening and weekend events, tired from the work load of the preceding five days.

3. *Shared meetings.* Shared meetings mean time and attention will be split between you and another unlucky victim. Neither party benefits as both agendas receive little more than nominal attention.

4. *Mealtime meetings.* When time is at a premium, mealtime meetings are often suggested. However, mealtime meetings represent constant interruptions by meal servers and passersby, as well as competition with the entertainment and work of eating.

Graciously decline mealtime meeting invitations and maneuver for a more advantageous time period.

Be Prepared

Not all timing opportunities can be anticipated in advance. Therefore, always be prepared for that split-second, unexpected opportunity to make yourself memorable. In order to be ready to dazzle them with your wonderfulness, the following preliminary work must be in place in advance of the timing opportunity.

1. *Know the facts.* Your knowledge base on the subject matter should be as deep as it is wide. Quote sources. Become the leading resource on the subject among your peers. Know more than they do, and let it be known in a respectful way.

2. *Have an opinion.* Opinions articulate a state of mind. Be prepared to state your opinion. The value of your opinion is determined by how frequently and how accurately your opinion correctly predicts outcomes. The more frequently your opinion is borne out, the more highly it will be regarded. Avoid the "let me think about" or "I'm not sure" responses that indicate an unformulated opinion. Possession of an opinion is evidence that you are able to think and apply knowledge as well as possess it.

3. *Make a difference.* Do something that will have a positive impact. Use your behavior and achievements to demonstrate the integrity of your opinions and values. Let your actions speak for you. You can use these actions to demonstrate a point or to show your passion for a point of view.

4. *Defend your values.* Personal values define who you are as an individual. Substantial personal values define a substantial person. Shifting and fleeting personal values define a less than substantial person, one who will shift and fleet. Defend your values and the actions that support those values at all costs. Defense of your values will repay you many times over in the future.

Creative Approaches to Timing Challenges

Often success lies in one's ability to manage the unmanageable. In this case, it means managing yourself onto the agenda of your boss, client, or prospective customer at an opportune time, creating the timing opportunity needed in order to allow your style and substance to be noticed, and appreciated.

Shrewd ways to manage your way onto the agenda include:

1. *Piggyback your project onto another that is already positioned.* Can your issue be considered a by-product of it? An influencer of it? A relative, contributor, or barrier to it?

2. *Schedule yourself on the boss's calendar.* Avoid asking for permission. Just do it. Work directly with the boss's secretary to find an advantageous calendar time, and slot yourself in.

3. *Take the initiative to schedule your presentation on the agenda of an appropriate meeting,* providing you are regularly in attendance at that meeting.

4. *Switch agenda places or meeting times with others who hold more desirable positions or times than you.* Then inform the secretary of the switch so that the master calendar reflects actual meeting times and topics.

5. *Arrange to "run into" your boss, client, or prospective customer*—in the parking lot, at a mutual meeting, in the hall, on the tennis court, or any other location where you will have five seconds to say, "Oh, Joe, glad I ran into you. I've been meaning to update you on the XYZ proposal. The timing is getting tight. Should we meet later this week?" This approach indicates that you are in control, and does not give the impression that you are needy for the meeting, but rather that the meeting is important to your targeted audience.

Managing the challenges of appropriate timing requires a sense of boldness and confidence in your acts. Go forward with certainty.

Communication

Although communication is not a unique element in the winning formula to make yourself memorable, it is a significant influencer of both the substance and style elements of the formula. The content of a communication reflects on the substance of your image, and the manner in which the communication is delivered reflects on the style you represent. For both elements, the dramatic importance of effective communication cannot be overstated. Consequently, one must focus on the qualities and characteristics of every communication effort.

An old Oriental proverb says, "The first ten words you say when meeting someone are more important than the next 10,000. If the first ten fail, 10,000 will not then avail."* Whether you say the words by using your vocal chords, or say the words with ink on paper, the principle is the same. Whether your audience is one or one thousand, the principles of effective communication remain the same. Your image and success depend on your ability to concisely and effectively deliver a message. There is no room for error, because words once spoken, or written, cannot be retrieved. In the following paragraphs the principles for effective individual conversations as well as for effective group communications are presented. These principles are universally adaptable to all forms of communication, verbal, written, and otherwise.

From the talent of America's most admired and successful speakers and executives, the examples in the following sections "Principles for Effective Group Communications" and "One-on-One Conversation Skills" can be compiled.

Principles for Effective Group Communications

1. *Know your audience*—their likes, dislikes, problem areas, and areas of pride.

2. *Avoid offensive comments and stay clear of highly sensitive subjects.* Sex, religion, and politics are on the "do not discuss" list of topics. You would do well to ferret out other sensitive areas and be prepared either to avoid them or to address them in the light of their sensitiveness. In any case, be aware of them.

3. *Know your material.* Refer as little as possible to note cards. Are all your facts verifiable? Be prepared to provide sources of information if you are asked.

4. *Arrive in advance.* One hour advance time is adequate to review the placement and working order of audiovisual equipment, microphone, props, and handouts, as well as to

---

*Elmer Wheeler, *How to Put Yourself Across* (New York: Bramhall House, 1962), p. 196.

become familiar with the surroundings in which you will be presenting.

5. *Meet the audience in advance.* Casually walk among audience members or greet them at the door. As you become familiar with some of the members, the nervousness you may be experiencing will dissolve.

6. *Arrange seating and supportive equipment.* Every seat should have a clear view of the speaker and visual aids. "Not a bad seat in the house" is the goal.

7. *Provide the host with an interesting introduction of yourself.* Make it entertaining as well as informative, and definitely brief.

8. *Fill the emptiness.* Use music in the room as a way of welcoming guests, as an interlude during breaks, and to signal the conclusion of the meeting. Choose music that fits the theme and mood of your topic.

9. *Check the basics of your personal appearance.* Zippers up?

10. *Check your state of mind.* Think of yourself as a winner!

11. *Review your goals.*

12. *Fill your mind with energy.* Ready, set, go!

13. *Clear your voice.* Keep a glass of lemon water on hand at the podium or near the stage with which to clear your throat and voice.

Creating a Memorable Presentation

Ralph Waldo Emerson once said, "To be simple is to be great." These words can be tested through observing hundreds of presentations to both personal and public audiences. A common set of simple elements consistently appears in the truly memorable, influential presentations.

Include as many of the following influential elements as possible into your personal presentation, no matter how large or small the audience, and assuredly you will be viewed a winner.

1. *Make passion work for you.* The most effective presenters clearly believe their message and want to share it. They express a sense of passion for the topic, a passion that the audience can feel.

2. *Use empowering and influential words.* Some of the most powerful words are:

valuable	purposeful	successful
unique	profitable	timely
championship	world-class	creative
intriguing	winning	strategies
solutions	excellent	advantage
new/improved	best of its kind	action-packed
cost-contained	efficient	convenient

What other words have currency with the people you are trying to influence? Use the language they are most tuned in to. Work as many of those words into your presentation as possible to ensure that your message is positively received.

3. *Make your message sensational.* Augment the message with an appeal to each of the five senses: sight, hearing, touch, taste, and smell. Let the audience experience your message through their senses. *Hear* the words. *See* props and supporting visual materials such as video clips, slides, overhead projections, and paper copies of key content elements. *Touch* a sample of the product or model. *Smell* the newness, and *taste* the sweetness of success. Get creative. The use of sensation helps the audience experience the message, thus making it more memorable.

4. *Use drama.* Drama creates an excitement within the audience that heightens the senses, and thus heightens expectations. If you choose to use drama, be aware that the presentation must meet heightened audience expectations in order to be judged successful and memorable.

5. *Exaggerate for effect.* Examples of extremes can be effective in making a point. The exaggerated state must be somewhat believable in order to avoid being labeled a joke. When using an extreme example to make a point, be prepared to support your comments or declarations with documented facts and examples in order to make the claim realistic.

6. *Involve your audience.* The probability of prolonged audience interest, support, and positive reaction is enhanced when its participation is built into the presentation. Members of the audience can be invited to take an active role, as in interactive discussions, or a passive role, as in posing questions or expressing their

opinions. Include numerous participatory components in each presentation.

7. *Speak positively.* Talk about qualities or aspects of people and any incidents relating to them in a positive light. Ascribe weaknesses and problems only to systems, processes, and non-human entities.

8. *Acknowledge all points of view.* There is no need to discuss alternative points of view, but acknowledging their existence makes you appear knowledgeable, forthright, and well-rounded. After briefly touching on them, return to your primary persuasive argument.

9. *Be honest.* Present the facts without distortion. Suspicion of dishonesty is a credibility and character killer.

10. *Prefer the simple to the complex.* Boil complex explanations down to their basic elements. Use easily understood analogies to make a point.

11. *Relate your presentation to audience experiences.* Translate key points into real life incidents and stories that bring the message closer to the audience's personal experiences.

12. *Add humor.* Demonstrate a sense of joy in your message. If you can tell a good joke that connects to your point, do so. If you are not good at joke telling, regardless of the quality of the joke, then don't tell it. Personal storytelling and quick-witted comments are as effective as a good joke. Don't take yourself too seriously. Roll with whatever opportunities arise to add laughter or to play on audience comments. Incorporate at least one humorous element in each presentation.

13. *Compliment the audience.* Refer to their intelligence, vision, values, insight, or other applicable attributes. The compliments should be sincere, not artificial.

14. *Thank the audience.* A gracious "thank you" to the audience for its time and attention, leaving people with words of encouragement, direction, and enthusiasm, establishes your control over the meeting and signals the conclusion of the presentation.

15. *Provide take-away gifts.* A small gift or token that the audience members take with them as they depart from the presentation is a perfect way to conclude the meeting, yet keep the experience alive in the audience's mind for some time to come.

Adding Quality to Your Presentation

The following characteristics and techniques are consistently found among top-rated executives and presenters as they interact with audiences of various sizes. The more of them you can include in your presentation the more memorable it will be.

1. *Use props.* A prop can be as simple as a piece of paper or as dynamic as a power tool. Props add entertainment value and help hold audience interest during the presentation. Pieces or parts of an item referred to in the topic presentation make good props, as do toys or other items that demonstrate a basic principle. Whatever you are going to talk about, have something to show that goes with your talk. In written communication, include samples of some kind for your reader to see, feel, or touch. If a sample is unavailable, include a photo or other type of illustration.

2. *Be animated.* Move about the stage or mingle with the audience. We are an animated people who are quickly bored with stillness. In written communication, various formatting changes and typefaces help to give the document more interest.

3. *Gesture.* Use your hands, arms, facial expressions, and body gestures to emphasize certain points and to assist in communicating your message. In written communication, use words to describe gestures or motions. For example, the words *moving, striking,* or *raising* are all useful in describing actions. "Moving along to the next idea..." is a good way to inject the notion of activity into what otherwise might be a stagnant communication.

4. *Control your voice tone and quality.* Nervousness tends to raise voice pitch, or add quiver to voice quality. This can be controlled by slowing your breathing and rate of speech. Then your voice pitch will return to normal. When you feel the need to recalibrate your voice tone, take a ten-second pause. It is long enough for your voice to readjust and short enough to be viewed as an ordinary pause by the audience.

5. *Articulate and enunciate.* Speak slowly. Effective speech is more deliberately and slowly delivered than the things we say in ordinary conversation. Articulate each syllable to clearly communicate the message. A slow, articulate delivery adds the element

of confidence to your image. Avoid using contractions such as *don't, can't,* or *wouldn't.* Rather, speak the two words, *do not, can not,* and *would not.* Practice making distinctions between *t, d,* and *p* sounds. Respond with "no" and "yes" rather than with "nah," "ya," or "ahha." In written communication, an economy of words is desirable. Write succinctly.

6. *Employ changes in voice volume.* Diversify voice volume to include the full range of normal, loud, and soft volumes in order to emphasize points or draw attention to something. In a written communication, use adjectives to describe the intensity of what your voice volume would be if you were verbally communicating the same message. For example, "I feel assured..." reflects a confident voice tone, while "It is imperative..." reflects a stronger, more intense voice volume.

7. *Pause for punch.* Use dramatic pauses to hold audience attention, and strategically set a concept apart from the balance of the message.

8. *Look at your audience.* Slowly rotate your head from side to side around the room in an effort to scan the entire audience, making all attendees feel included in the message. Make eye contact with several people throughout the room.

9. *Stick to time frames.* Respect your allocated time. Extensions beyond scheduled time frames are annoying, and diminish the total effect of the presentation. Finish early if possible. It's a pleasant surprise to the audience, and makes you look more organized than if you run overtime. In written communications, keep the message as concise as possible. Less is often more.

10. *Appeal to audience emotions.* Emotional links are fundamental to creating a memorable experience. The stronger the emotional link to your audience is, the more memorable the event will be. Common emotional links include such things as caring, compassion, safety, personal growth and development, children, peace, the human race, values, and respect. Materialistic appeals for such things as money are far less memorable than they would be with a corresponding emotional link.

11. *Ignore distractions.* Common distractions such as latecomers, coughers, gigglers, and other noisy interruptions should not be viewed as personal attacks but rather as common

occurrences. Ignore them and proceed as if they did not exist. Attention paid to a distraction breaks the flow of communication and audience attention.

One-on-One Conversation Skills

The preparation and presentation techniques discussed in this chapter are applicable to any type or size of audience, to a professional colleague, a prospective client, a family member, or a friend. However, additional, special skills are needed to make yourself memorable in personal conversations, in which listening often gives you the advantage over speaking.

1. *Listen more than you speak.* The art of good conversation is to let the other person do most of the talking. Ask questions and note the answers. Note taking is a way of communicating, "Your message is important. I want to get this down." As a form of body language, it makes the speaker like you. In written communications you can engage the reader in a conversation of sorts by including questions and soliciting opinions or points of view within the document.

2. *Get your audience to draw "natural" conclusions.* Through the process of information exchange and the prompting of key questions, it is possible to have your audience draw the conclusions you desire them to come to. Self-persuasion is an effective, lasting persuasion that leaves the person with a satisfied feeling at the end of the conversation.

3. *Don't let personal weaknesses or biases show.* Everybody loves a winner, and weaknesses, though natural, detract from the winning image you are creating. Avoid the use of self-deprecating comments or language that indirectly or directly puts you in a down position. For example, "I'm not good enough," "I don't think I can handle that," or "I'm not organized enough" are comments routinely made with little thought given to their negative implications. Never affirm a negative.

4. *Use positive language.* Express negative messages in a positive manner. For example, if the results of a work process are less than expected, the positive approach would sound something like this: "As you know, we have encountered unexpected

challenges, and although the results are not as positive as we had hoped for, progress was made." How you say it is as important as what you say.

5. *Make connections that you can refer to.* Even if the connections are distant, you can use them to command attention and steer the conversation. Having met someone influential, gone somewhere special, or experienced something connected to the conversation gives you a relaxed command of the situation and establishes a communication link between you and others. "No kidding, you spent time in Chicago, too…" or "When you visited with them, did you notice their outstanding collection of…?" are examples of conversational gambits that casually link people together.

6. *Use positive body language.* Lean forward and nod positively to indicate your feelings of compassion, understanding, and encouragement to continue the conversation.

7. *Ask opinions and advice.* To be asked for one's opinion or advice is viewed as an honor. Thus, to ask someone for his opinion is to bestow some level of honor upon him.

8. *Use "we" rather than "I."* "We" is an inclusive concept that indicates the representation of more than one person, a more influential representation. "We" also avoids the trap of talking about yourself, because it inherently implies the inclusion of others. When talking about a problem or conflict, never use the words *you* or *your,* which suggest finger pointing, and will therefore raise defenses in the other person. Bud Norris, retired executive of Upjohn Healthcare Services and one of the best communicators we've encountered, said that leaders must become "masters of conversation."

Personal conversations are an excellent way to build relationships. They allow people to befriend one another, break down barriers, build relationships, and show versatility. To build a base of relationships, tactically plan to engage in as many personal conversations as possible. Practice conversation and presentation skills in each aspect of your daily routine. Conversation is a learned skill that progresses with practice.

How to Kill a Message

There are but a few instantly deadly ways to kill your message. Whether it is a professional presentation or a personal conversation, any one of the following could be considered a poison pill.

- Talking about yourself
- Bragging
- Using too much technical jargon
- Talking down to your audience
- Making it hard to hear or see your message
- Larding your talk with clichés
- Making claims that are unbelievable
- Presenting your topic from your point of view only
- Appearing messy, dull, or unorganized

Part Two

Above the Crowd: Memory-Making Strategies

"People will sit up and take notice of you if you will sit up and take notice of what makes them sit up and take notice."

—*Frank Romer*

Endless interactions, conversations, and activities dominate our daily lives. Of the many people and events we experience, only a few become memorable, and stand the test of time. These are the events and people we can easily and vividly recollect. Their recall awakens emotions within us as we relive them in memory.

What is it that makes these people or events memorable? What traits are common to all memorable events? Is there a formula for creating a memorable event or building a memorable image? Answers to these questions reveal the strategies for making yourself memorable, for enriching any relationship you choose to target.

Observation and study indicate that there are five strategies for making yourself memorable (see Figure P-2). Individually, or in combination, each of these strategies has the potential for creating memorable images and events.

Figure P-2 Strategies for making yourself memorable.

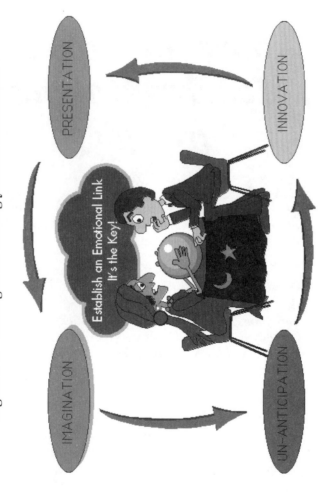

2

Innovation: A Memory-Making Strategy

"Creativity [is] letting go of certainties."
—Gail Sheehy

The massive volume of innovation and change affecting our daily lives has become overwhelming. New medical practices extend our years, and new computer software that amazes is soon out of date. An elderly friend says, "Nothing I once knew now exists. I don't know this world." So much change and innovation within one lifetime. In the midst of this swirling change, how can one stand out?

Innovation is the primary cause of great volumes of change, and it is also a primary strategy for making yourself memorable. As evidenced by the massive amount of change we are experiencing, there is an extraordinary number of innovations. However, only a few of them will become memorable. What causes some to become memorable, and others not?

There are two driving characteristics an innovation must have in order to be memorable (see Figure 2-1).

The first characteristic is the perceived value of what the innovation provides to people. People assign a value to everything. Think of the common question, "Was it worth it?" We hear this asked frequently, one person asking another for a judgment on the value of something. Innovations that provide great value to people become memorable, whereas innovations that provide negligible value pass by and are soon forgotten. Well-known innovations such as the automobile, airplane, and computer are

Figure 2-1   The two characteristics of memorable innovations.

> • **SUSTAINED ATTENTION**
> • **A SENSE OF VALUE**

thought to provide great value, and therefore they and their inventors become celebrated.

The second characteristic needed to make an innovation memorable is that it sustains substantial audience attention and interest. The greater the level of interest and attention, the more memorable it will be. The very nature of innovation, being something new, perhaps never before conceived, or perhaps conceived but only now realized, commands a certain degree of initial public attention and interest. To the extent that the innovation can sustain this level of attention and interest, or increase it, it will become memorable. To the extent that the initial attention and interest are small or rapidly declining, it will not be memorable. The challenge, then, is to manage the level of attention, interest, and value that the targeted audience gives to the innovation.

Why Innovation Is Attractive

People are drawn to innovative ideas, processes, and items for four major reasons:

1. *Intrigue.* It's totally new, previously unconceived. There's a sense of curiosity about it and a desire to explore this alien terrain. Computers fit this description. People are intrigued by what these machines can do, and how quickly they can do it.

2. *Fascination.* How does it work? What does it do? Why does it work the way it does? Endless questions are born out of fascination and the desire to know more. For example, people are fascinated by the facial creams and medical processes that claim to repair wrinkles and reverse the outward damage of the aging process.

3. *Excitement.* It's new, never before achieved, different from what has become routine. Anticipation builds. Will it do what it is expected to do? Early space exploration is an example of innovation that attracted interest through the excitement it generated.

4. *Needs and/or desires.* How can this innovation serve my needs or fill my desires? Antibiotics serve mankind's survival need, and automobiles answer the desire for mobility; both are innovations that attract and sustain audience interest because they meet long-standing needs or desires.

Of the four reasons people are attracted to innovations, "need" is the one driving factor that determines the value placed on the innovation. The greater the need for the innovation is, the higher the value people will place on it, and the more attention and interest it will garner, thus the more memorable it will be. When the value of the need declines, the state of being memorable will also begin to fade.

Regardless of the reasons people are initially attracted to an innovation, to become memorable the innovation must eventually migrate into the category of "needs and desires."

Opportunities for Innovation

Some people are natural innovators. Quickly and easily they see ways and opportunities to improve upon the present. Others want to innovate, but do not know where to focus their energies. The following concepts, adapted in part from Peter Drucker's book *Innovation and Entrepreneurship,* describe seven primary categories of opportunities for innovation, situations that would naturally call for innovation. Apply these concepts to your environment to pinpoint possible opportunities for valued innovations.

1. *Incongruity.* Incongruity occurs when there is a difference between what reality is and what we think reality should be. The innovation opportunity occurs when you create something that will bring current reality into line, or congruity, with what we want reality to be. For example, we should be able to enjoy sunshine without the risk of sunburn or pain. Hence, the creation of sunscreen, which allows us to do just that.

2. *Process need.* Process opportunities occur when there is a need to improve something in order to succeed. For example, in order to improve customer service by reducing the waiting time for checkout at gasoline stations, Mobil Oil created a new process to take customer credit card payment at the pump—a process improvement that reduces waiting time for credit card customers.

3. *Unexpected success or failure.* We might call this innovation by accident. Innovation is not always planned. The unexpected success or failure of some unplanned event could cause one to innovate in order to prevent future failures, or to innovate in order to reinforce and multiply future successes.

4. *Fun.* People of all ages innovate for fun and self-entertainment. Making changes to routine and common approaches makes the usual unusual, the common uncommon, and the boring more interesting. Children combine innovation and play to create new games. Adults combine innovation and work to find new ways of doing old tasks more efficiently and enjoyably.

5. *Problem solving.* Problem solving through innovation often creates heroes and legends. Two types of problems have hero-making potential: (1) an immediate crisis; and (2) a long-term problem situation. The M factor (memory-making factor) in a crisis is its perceived "extreme" negative nature, and the implications of the situation. Therefore, resolution of a crisis has hero-making potential. An innovative resolution adds the additional M factor of "firsts" to the solution, increasing its probability of becoming a memorable event. A case in point would be a hiker in the woods whose leg is badly injured. His companion innovatively combines tree branches and grasses to devise a splint and crutch, making it possible to get the injured person to safety. Innovative problem solving turned the companion into a hero in the eyes of the one in crisis in the same way that solving long-term problems can make you a legend in the eyes of those benefiting from the innovation. Inventors of the microwave oven, cellular telephone, and home computer are heroes to working mothers. The inventor of the polio vaccine is a hero to all those who would otherwise have suffered or died from the debilitating disease.

6. *Survival.* To survive in a quality state requires defense against enemies that attack. Disease, famine, natural disasters,

and greed are but a few of the evolving enemies of human survival. Constant innovation fends off aggressors and spells survival. Innovation of antibiotics that fight against deadly diseases means the survival of a species, and innovation of artificial body parts extends human life. Some day there will be an innovative solution for cancer. Innovation born out of the instinct for survival is the work of heroes.

7. *Competitive Advantage.* A competitive advantage is something that makes one more likely to win than another, however winning is defined. It is something extra that is uniquely possessed by one competitor. Innovation is what competitive advantages are made of. People innovate in order to win.

In a competitive environment, innovation is the key to success. Being the first to offer a valued new feature or product is to be in a more prominent and prosperous position than that of being second. Subsequent product entries into a market where strong innovations reside beg for an expensive battle against the memorable image that the original innovator has acquired. For example, Macintosh computers, introduced in 1984, were the first to innovate a friendly interface, thus creating a valued invention and making it easy for customers to use the product. When Microsoft introduced Windows 95 into the same market eleven years later, it had to spend $300 million to offset the earlier memorable and competitive advantage Macintosh enjoyed.

To the extent that the targeted audience retains a substantial level of interest in, and assigns a significant value to, an innovation generated out of these seven categories of opportunity, the innovation will sustain its memorable status.

The Process for Generating Innovative Ideas

For some people, innovative idea generation is a natural, unbridled thinking process that generates a quick set of workable ideas. For others, idea generation is a deliberate work process that uses more formal steps to reach the same goal.

The following formal step-by-step process is provided to assist those who wish to innovate but need some additional direction. This process works in coordination with each of the seven previously discussed opportunities for innovation.

1. *Know in detail the components of the present process, problem, or dilemma.* Understand what the problem is and what it is not, and isolate all factors contributing to the situation.

2. *Identify the goal in plain terms.* What is it that you want this innovation to accomplish? What are the characteristics of the desired end product? Play the game "It would be great if..." to generate new and creative goals.

3. *Brainstorm unconditionally and nonjudgmentally on ways to solve the problem.* Use the five Ws—who, what, when, where, why—to generate ideas:

   1. *Who* would be affected, *who* might be interested, and *who* would benefit.
   2. *What* we do.
   3. *Where* it would happen.
   4. *When* it would happen.
   5. *Why* it would happen.

Change the elements of the five Ws to create new ideas to add to your brainstorming list. For example, change the population of people who might be interested, or where it might happen, and alternative ideas will be generated. Continue the process with the five Ws until all possibilities are exhausted.

4. *Assess alternatives.* Look for approaches having the greatest probability of success. What would generate the strongest and longest audience attention span? What would have the greatest perceived value to the target audience?

5. *Create an implementation plan.* List the resources needed and possible suppliers. Determine your timetable and identify who is accountable for the various implementation phases. Establish measures for feedback and standards to determine success.

6. *Go and do it.*

Fading Sizzle: The Aging Innovation

Nothing is eternal. Every person, place, or thing has a life span. This includes innovations. In our throwaway society we continually ask, "What have you done for me lately?" as we seek new ideas and newer innovations.

Major league pitcher Carl Hubbell summed it up best when he said, "A fellow doesn't last long on what he has done. He's got to keep on delivering as he goes along." An innovation retains its memorable status only to the extent that it continues to renew itself by virtue of improvements. Innovations have a life span whose length is determined by how quickly a new innovation is generated to replace the present one, or how quickly the targeted audience loses interest in, or sees a declining value in, the innovation. This time factor can be a matter of days, years, or generations.

For example, for years Mercedes-Benz kept its auto products fresh with twenty or more new improvements or innovations annually, thus prolonging the life of the product and avoiding the aging innovation problem. Then, to the surprise of many, a new competitor, the Lexus automobile, entered the fray. Lexus products included all the Mercedes-Benz innovative designs plus one more key innovative feature—a customer price substantially lower than that of the Mercedes-Benz. Lexus thereby outinnovated Mercedes.

It happens. The life span of an innovation begins to fade when one or more of the following circumstances exist:

1. The innovation moves from being extraordinary to ordinary, from uncommon to common, from unusual to routine.
2. A newer, better innovation is announced that replaces or improves upon the original innovation.
3. The personal features that initially made the innovative person, place, or thing valuable now become weak or extinct.

When Is Innovation a Good Strategy to Use?

Innovation is the strategy of choice to make yourself memorable when:

1. *You want to be different from the rest.* In total, there are few innovators in our population but an overwhelming majority of

users of innovation. This lack of innovative talent causes people to use the few innovative ideas that have been generated. Most people borrow concepts, behaviors, and applications that others have created and use them past the burnout point, continuing until the next innovation arrives. Consequently, what we see and hear from most people are commonplace, used and reused approaches, attitudes, or opinions, lacking originality or any further development. Innovation makes you distinguishably different in a copycat environment.

2. *Everything else has failed.* When alternatives are ineffective, innovation will solve the problem by creating a new solution that works.

3. *You desire something more, something different.* When what is available is not good enough, you will have to create something that is.

4. *You want to prove a point.* If current examples will not prove your point, then create an example that will make the argument convincing. Innovate.

With the innovation strategy, the resulting innovation, rather than the innovator, is most likely to be memorable. This is because it is the innovation rather than the innovator that routinely provides value to the target audience. The innovator may become memorable by association with the innovation when:

- The innovation becomes a household word.
- The innovation radically changes the way people live.
- The innovation affects a large population of people.

If you are willing to accept a memorable status by virtue of association with your innovation, then this is a strategy that can universally be applied in personal or professional situations.

Preserving a Memorable Status

Innovation is a short-lived strategy for building an image or having a memorable item or event. Once introduced, an innovation begins to age and fade over time, requiring ongoing attention in order to preserve its memorable status. There are four techniques for preserving the memorable status of an innovation:

1. *New and improved versions or models.* New components are added to or replace the original model and thereby sustain the memorable product image status. An innovation remains memorable only for the period of time from notable introduction until the delivery of the next notable generation, version, or concept.

2. *Originality.* The element of originality contributes to sustaining the memorable status of an innovation because it represents the first of its kind. Improvements and subsequent new versions do not detract from the memorability of the original product. For example, recall the original shape of the Coca-Cola bottle. Curvy and distinct. Although there have been numerous Coca-Cola packaging innovations since the original bottle, the original product package remains memorable.

3. *Retaining an attentive population.* A memorable status lives on only as long as the person experiencing that status lives on or passes it on. Passing on the stories and experiences of people, places, or things that have gone before us is one way of maintaining the life and memorable quality of the event. As long as there is an audience interested in hearing the story of a memorable person, product, or event, the memorable status remains.

4. *Periodic recall.* The memorable status of an innovation lasts only as long as the lifetime of the people who use or experience that innovation. When the population of people using an innovative idea expires, so goes its memorable status. Therefore, preserving a memorable status requires constant work and periodic recall in order to retain the original vividness. Once the life of a person or innovation expires, it is likely that the memorable status will fade with it unless there are planned memory prompters, things that recall a memorable event or person and rejuvenate the vividness of the past.

There are a number of ways to help preserve memorable moments, people, and things. No one preservation method is foolproof or complete. The combination of as many of these approaches as possible creates the strongest probability of successfully passing today's memories onto later generations.

1. *Photographs.* Photos provide a visual reminder of the person, place, or thing to be remembered. Everlasting, photos and videos keep the details of the past intact. Keep photos in dry dark storage in order to preserve the vividness of the color. Exposure to sunlight fades colors over time.

2. *Journals.* Keeping a journal is a personal process of writing down daily one's feelings, activities, or reactions to current events. Written references provide details about and insights into how previous generations lived and thought. Even more than photos, which capture people and events at a specific point in time, journals reveal the emotional responses of people to events and experiences. Together, the combination of photos and journals can resurrect the past.

3. *Stories.* Stories of personal experience are a special way of sharing an event, reliving the event, and teaching others. More than a photo or a journal, the storyteller colors the experience by enlisting the use of all the senses to describe every detail. Somehow, stories magically evolve over time. They are never retold with exactly the same detail.

4. *Poetry.* Poetry is the artistic telling of a story, from a unique personal perspective, yet described or expressed in a few well conceived lines. Bold and blunt, or intentionally ambiguous, poetry is a means by which artists give the outline of a story, but leave it to the reader to fill in the implications.

5. *Audiotapes.* Within recent years, audiotape technology and equipment has become inexpensive and commonplace, making it an excellent resource for eternally preserving verbal communication—or at least until the audiotape player is out-innovated. Audiotapes preserve conversations, emotions, and detailed circumstances in your personal voice. In some ways, audiotaping is better than a photo or journal because an actual element of the living person is preserved on the tape.

6. *Reminders.* Memories fade as time wears on, but reminders of the past help keep friends and events vivid. They act as a battery charger. Pieces of physical evidence are good reminders. Ticket stubs, menus, invitations, and news clippings all serve this purpose. A rock from the beach where you vacationed, painted with the event and date on it, or a piece of lumber from your house, signed and dated with the address on it, are free

and fun examples of reminders. You will often see strange items prominently displayed in executive offices. They are usually reminders of some past event—for example, a brick from the original building, a copy of the first business transaction the company conducted, or framed publicity stories of some past event. These are free and effective reminders of the past.

Artificial Innovation

Claiming that something is "new" and "improved" is a common but weak attempt to extend the life of an innovation. A "new and improved" detergent is generally not appreciably newer or improved, at least not to the extent that it would warrant privileges that come with an innovation. These are efforts to artificially extend the life of the original innovation, which has declining memorability value.

As a strategy, artificial innovation is a weak, nondescript, leechlike approach used by those who appreciate the value of true innovation but are unable to create it. Such attempts generate unfavorable feelings among users and consumers that carry over to and tend to efface the previously memorable qualities the truly innovative product once had. Steer clear of artificial innovation as a strategy associated with your work or efforts.

3

Imagination:
A Memory-Making
Strategy

"Always remember that this whole thing started with a mouse."
—*Walt Disney*

Everybody has one, yet few of us use it. Imagination. What is it? How do you make it work? Like a rare spice, imagination is sometimes best used sparingly and in appropriate recipes or circumstances in order to become memorable. But, like Hoover Dam, it sometimes must come pouring forth in huge quantities. Too much and it could be off base, childish and inappropriate, disruptive to other fine qualities you have to offer. In appropriate doses, it is the difference between routine and uncommon thinking.

Imagination is a unique quality of the mind, the precursor to innovation. It is the ability to visualize and see, through the mind's eye, what is not yet there. It is the ability to create what is not, from nothing. It is a tool we use every day, but not necessarily in effective ways.

There are four primary ways in which imagination can be used in personal and professional life to create a memorable image (see Figure 3-1).

Let's look at each of the ways imagination can be used to create something memorable.

Figure 3-1   Four ways to use imagination.

- **FUN & DELIGHT**
- **VISUALIZATION**
- **EXPLORATION**
- **TEACHING**

Fun and Delight

When it brings a smile to your face and makes you feel good, it's a delight. When it is something that you enjoy immensely, it's fun. When it brings smiles to your face and is something you immensely enjoy, it is fun and delight.

Not all fun and delightful characteristics or experiences become memorable. Some are short-lived, one-time creations. Others go on to become memories. What makes the difference?

There are seven qualities that contribute to making imaginative fun and delight memorable.

1. *The intensity of originality of the imaginary character or event.* The more elements of originality there are to the character or event, the more likely it is to become memorable.

2. *Sensory impacts.* The greater the number of senses (sight, sound, touch, taste, and smell) the character or event involves, the more memorable it will be.

3. *Ease of recall.* The easier it is to recall the character or event, the more memorable it is likely to become. A prominently used technique for improving ease of recall is the three Rs: rhythms, rhymes, and repeats. Messages that use rhyming lyrics and rhythmic flow of words are more easily and rapidly recalled than those that do not. Also, the more frequently the rhymes and rhythms are presented (meaning the greater number of times we are exposed to the message), the more likely they will be remembered.

4. *Animation.* Characters and events that "come to life" and interact with you are more memorable than stationary ones. The more animated and interactive the character or situation is, the more memorable it is likely to be.

5. *Grand scaling.* The grander the scaling of the character or event is, the more likely it will become memorable. The imaginative character of Mickey Mouse, for instance, is available in more sizes and formats than just the original cartoon. His imaginative character has been transferred to hundreds, perhaps thousands, of products: stuffed animals, full-length films, school supplies, clothing. He is massively and frequently exposed. He has presented on a grand scale.

The McDonald's All American Marching Band, a creative event generating fun and delight, is not composed of fifteen average band members but rather of one hundred or more band members from all over the United States. Their musical performances are extensive, and the quality of their music is exceptional. It is a fun and delightful product created and presented on a grand scale.

6. *Rarity.* The rarer the experience is, the more memorable it is likely to be. Rarity can refer to the availability of the character or experience, or it can refer to the number of exposures to the character or experience. If you've experienced Disneyland only one time, that one rare experience will be more memorable than if you are a frequent visitor.

Use the six qualities that contribute to making imaginative fun and delight memorable in order to transform personal situations into memorable ones. Consider the case of my unique and memorable marriage proposal delivered with fun and delight. Not only was the experience imaginative, delightful, and fun, it was also unexpected.

With no prearranged date on the calendar, the hopeful groom-to-be arrives at my house dressed in the costume of a knight in shining armor, complete with shield and sword. Playing out the role, he does not ring the doorbell, but rather calls to me from below the balcony window. Hearing a strange beckoning call, I go to the balcony railing only to see a crowd of neighbors gathering (where are they when you really need them?!) There he stands in full costume, reciting lines of poetry, and swinging his sword and shield. Imagine my surprise! At the end of the poetic recital, he drops to one knee and softly asks, "Will you marry me?" The crowd applauds.

Imaginative? Yes. Fun? Yes. Unexpected? Yes. Memorable? Yes.

An Audience For Fun and Delight

Imagination as a tool to create memorable fun and delightful experiences is most frequently employed with childhood audiences. Rarely do corporate entities indulge in widespread imaginative fun and delight. Those that do, however, create a memorable corporate image for themselves with both customers and employees. Case in point, McDonald's has a Vice President of Fun, the All American Marching Band, playlands, happy meals, Hamburglar and friends. They conduct their business in a way that is laced with fun and delight. Hardees, a competing organization, has none of these things. When you ask the kids where they want to go for lunch, are they going to choose: McDonald's or Hardee's?

People and organizations who create imaginative fun and delight become memorable. What can you do to inject light-hearted fun and delight into your working environment while benefiting the organization?

Visualization Through Imagination

Some people have the uncanny ability to project the future based on present facts and trends. They can think past the present, considering what the trends mean for the future— visualizing what is yet to be. When minds are encouraged to expand thinking beyond present known boundaries and to "imagine," or conceptualize, what todays' facts and trends mean for tomorrow, then the power of imagination is used to visualize.

Some people visualize, yet neither they nor their vision become memorable. Other people visualize and both they and their vision become memorable. What makes the difference? Why are some memorable and others not?

There are three qualities consistently found in memorable visionaries. All three qualities must be present in order for the vision and its author to be memorable.

1. *They must envision a dramatic change.* The visualization must represent something that is thought to be dramatically different from the present.
2. *They must be influential.* They must have the power to modify or neutralize future negatives before they occur, thus eliminating barriers that could interfere with the actualization of the vision. At the same time, they must have the power to harness and magnify future positives, using them to bring the vision to reality.
3. *They must be accurate.* The projected vision of the future must actually come to pass as envisioned.

Exploration Through Imagination

To explore is to go where you've never been before, to inquisitively seek out something. Exploration through imagination allows you to:

1. Combine and extend the various dimensions of reality.
2. Create the maximum number of alternatives.
3. Evaluate the alternatives without materializing them.

By opening up the mind to suggestions and ideas, and banning preconceptions and jaded judgments that accumulate with time and experience, one can play out, in the imagination, all the possible scenarios of the various combinations, allowing an exploration of both new and old ideas that others have discarded. It is a breaking away from dominant group thinking and a move toward open thinking as a way of making yourself memorable. Open thinking is characterized by:

1. *A ban on prejudgments.* All ideas are fair ideas to be investigated.
2. *A break from group thinking.*

3. *An introduction to possibility thinking,* that is, perpetually asking the question, "why not?"
4. *A structured evaluative process.*

At the point where exploration through imagination generates a valuable new discovery, or salvages a valuable oversight from previous thinking, the individual and the discovery will become memorable.

Imagination as a Teaching Tool

Imagination as a teaching tool has the potential to make both the teacher and the lesson learned memorable. Because no one person ever possess all the knowledge and wisdom he or she needs, learning is a lifelong process, and teaching provides a lifelong opportunity to make yourself memorable.

Use of the imagination as a teaching tool is a nonoffensive, participatory way for adults and children to learn about relationships, dynamics, and projected outcomes. Lessons are taught and messages are communicated through use of the technique of imaginary predictions.

In this technique, the role of the teacher is to outline situational facts in a clear and concise manner, then ask the student to imagine what might happen if the behavior or circumstances do not change; or what might happen if certain specific elements are introduced into the situation. By painting a relational picture between present facts and imaginary circumstances, one can explore and visualize what the future might look like, what the consequences might be.

A simple lesson can turn into a memorable event. After numerous failed attempts to instill in my son a sense of the importance of safety on the street, my son continued to ride his bicycle with no regard for the danger of passing cars. Then the opportunity to teach through imaginary predictions presented itself. Pointing out a crushed animal on the roadside, I posed the question to him, "What would have happened to you if that car had hit you instead of this animal?" I could see in his face, as he processed that question, that the message was finally getting through. The lesson would be remembered.

There are two circumstances in which imagination as a teaching tool will generate a memorable result. They are:

1. When what is learned is highly valued by the student, when it is enlightening, informative, or useful.
2. When the learning occurs through self-directed discovery.

The more highly valued the lesson learned is, the more likely the teacher and event will become memorable.

Unleashing the Powers of Imagination

Walt Disney once said, "If you can dream it, you can do it." Imagination is the source of your dreams. It is a unique core characteristic around which a strong personal or professional image can be built. Directed use of vivid imagination will cause you to be viewed as a valuable, creative, open thinker. Creative problem solving, imaginative advertising campaigns and sales presentations, or insightful visionary approaches to leadership and action are all examples of the use of imagination that will set you apart from the crowd.

Imagination that is properly channeled has the potential to assist you in many ways. Consider using the power of imagination to:

- Communicate an abstract concept.
- Venture into the unknown.
- Reduce stress. (Daydreaming is a stress-free escape.)
- Create a competitive advantage.
- Visualize a goal.
- Practice an act or speech.
- Do what you thought you never could do.
- Make life fun and delightful.

Finally, always remember what the twentieth century's most influential scientist and thinker once said:

"Imagination is more important than knowledge."

4

Presentation: A Memory-Making Strategy

"Put it before them briefly so they will read it, clearly so they will appreciate it, picturesquely so they will remember it and, above all, accurately so they will be guided by its light."

—Joseph Pulitzer

According to Webster's, presentation is "the setting forth of something for the attention of the mind." Thinking in broad, unbound terms, there are many forms of presentation. The presentation of an idea. The presentation of information as in a seminar or speech. The presentation of food, as at a meal. Or the presentation of a gift.

Because of the rushed style of today's living, the presentation aspect of events is frequently cut short, robbing the event of much of its value. For example, the common prepackaged eat-and-run meal sacrifices the beauty and relaxation characteristic of even a simple sit-down meal where the presentation of food from soup to dessert can be made interesting and artistic. It need not be elaborately presented for the presentation to be memorable. The memory-making quality is not in the elaboration of the presentation but in the quality and distinctiveness of it. Any routine activity can be turned into a memorable event through the application of a memory-making presentation.

Eating can be an event. Imagine a theme-based meal. Various colors of food artistically arranged, different utensils for each type of food, drinks coordinated with and complementing food tastes, different types of plates for each course, a few decorations, and perhaps a centerpiece that is edible. A simple meal made memorable and certainly more enjoyable.

Gift giving is an activity largely conducted in nonimaginary, uneventful ways. But it need not be just handing something over from one person to another. Drama, action, passion— emotions of some kind need to be involved in the delivery to make it fun and memorable. For example, you could deliver the gift in a costume representing a character that relates to the gift for a fun and uninhibited approach. The simplest of gifts can be made memorable by the creation of a whole presentation. The delivery of a gift or message can be as influential and important as the gift itself in terms of making a favorable impression. The stage must be set. The story behind the search for the gift and the connection between the gift giver and the idea for the gift are shared. A picture starts to develop in your audience's mind. Anticipation and excitement builds. Finally, the gift is delivered.

The packaging of the gift or message must be unique. Rather than relying solely on the gift to be memorable, add the extra punch of creative packaging to make the presentation a complete experience. You will want something more than a standard cardboard box. Consider a ceramic container, a balloon, coffee can, piece of crystal, anything but the standard delivery container.

Whether for business, pleasure, or social purposes, the effectiveness of imaginative, vivid, whole-experience presentations should not be underestimated.

Build upon each of the five steps to effective personal and professional presentations to create a memorable experience (see Figure 4-1).

Figure 4-1   The five steps to effective presentations.

- **INTRODUCTION**
- **BEGINNING**
- **CORE CONTENT**
- **CONCLUSION**
- **ENCORE**

Introduction

The introduction is the attention-getting step of a presentation, the time and place where anticipation and excitement about the event are built. It is the famous moment of first impression.

Like the hors d'oeuvre or antipasto preceding the entrée in a restaurant, the introduction is a brief descriptive step that sets the stage for the first direct encounter with the audience. Do not confuse the introductory stage of a presentation with the introduction of the speaker or main event.

In a business environment, the introduction is also the attention-getting descriptive step. Audience attention is being sharply focused on the geographical space where the presentation is to occur, and first impressions are being made.

A recent example of a highly effective introductory step for a presentation occurred in Las Vegas. A large ballroom was the setting for this conference and nearly a thousand people were in attendance. The conference was scheduled to begin at 2:00 P.M. Until 1:59 P.M. the doors to the ballroom were closed and locked so that conference attendees could not enter. Inside the ballroom a marching band was assembling to kick off the main event. At exactly 2:00 P.M., the doors to the ballroom were flung open to the sound and sight of the band playing "When the saints come marching in!"

Attention was immediately focused on the band, located at the front of the ballroom, just behind where the speaker would be standing. Energy and excitement filled the air, and a successful introduction to the presentation had occurred.

When the introductory step is neglected, and the speaker is brought forward with an unknown amount of enthusiasm from the audience, the overall effect is much less than it could have been. Conversely, when the introductory step is managed correctly, the probability of a successful and memorable presentation is much higher.

Beginning

The beginning, like the opening toast of a celebration, is the first direct encounter between the presenter and the audience. A successful connection between the audience and the beginning message of the presentation is essential.

The degree to which you can connect directly affects the extent to which the audience responds to the message. Greater connectedness buys greater audience response. Musicians connect with their audience through musical lyrics. Strong, broad audience identification with the song makes it a hit. When the story, values, or emotional message of a film connect with the audience, a hit movie is born. As the presenter, when your message connects with the audience, you will be a hit.

There are three personal qualities that the presenter must possess in order to connect with the audience. They are likability, trustworthiness, and an emotional connection on either a personal level or through the message. The stronger these personal qualities are, the greater the audience connection to the presenter will be.

Charismatic presenters build likability with the audience in the first precious moments of the encounter by befriending them, pointing out the importance of their role, and then building bridges between themselves and the audience as they go along.

The following universally workable phrases serve as appropriate introductory remarks:

"I am delighted to be here today because…"
"As I look out on this audience, I see a number of familiar and friendly faces."
"[*City name*] is one of my favorite places. It is good to be here, and it is a great honor to be with this group."
"I've waited a long time for this opportunity…"
"We are gathered here today because we share…"
"This is a great audience because…"
"I knew this was a great audience when…"
"This is going to be a wonderful experience because. . ."

If you want to create your own bridges to familiarity and likability, the following guidelines will help:

1. *Tell audience members how delighted you are to be with them, and why.* Starting phrases like, "I am so delighted to be here," are shallow and ineffective unless you tell the audience why you are delighted to be with them. Finish the sentence with, "because…"

2. *Compliment them on their choice of topics, themes, or speakers for the meeting.*

3. *Show respect.* Refer to their intelligence, insight, achievements, or other favorable qualities.

4. *Identify an existing link.* This would be some form of understanding, possibly a common emotion or passion that you share with the audience. The following examples are universally workable.

> "I understand the many challenges…"
> "We have the opportunity to build…"
> "It is our common goal to…"
> "It is our collective effort to…"

5. *Use inclusive pronouns.* "We" and "our" connect you to, and include you in, the audience's world.

6. *Do something fun for or with the audience.* Use props. Keep them simple to make basic points. Toys and childhood items are adaptable, fun-like props that can be used to illustrate a point.

7. *Give something to each audience member.* Gift giving is the custom of people who like one another. A take-home gift of some kind that relates to the topic, theme, or objective of the meeting is a good choice. The gift serves as a future reminder of the presentation and leaves the audience with a good feeling.

Building credibility and audience trust takes more time than creating likability. A certain degree of trust is initially bestowed on you based on the level of your credentials. Strong credentials may generate an initial trust, but that level of trust requires further substantiation and development in the early minutes of the presentation.

Further credibility and trust are created when:

- An extended level of factual, relevant knowledge is exhibited.
- Courage is exhibited by daring to state the obvious, unfavorable facts that others know but avoid talking about.
- Something personal about yourself or family is shared with the audience, thus creating a feeling of openness, vulnerability, and "trustability."

- The communication exchange is candid, direct, completely honest, yet respectful.

Core Content

The core content, like the entrée in a restaurant, represents the meat and potatoes of your message, the reason why the audience has gathered. Effective management of the core content, as well as the delivery style of the presentation, directly influences the degree to which the audience adapts to the message, is persuaded by the message, or enjoys the message. The following prescriptions ensure greater receptivity to your message.

1. *Be honest with the audience.* Air the shortcomings of your presentation, but in a manner that makes them seem negligible.

2. *Adjust the message to fit the audience.* Emphasize points of interest and concern or any emotional links that audience members can quickly identify with. You may also be able to adjust the delivery style of your message to the specific type of audience. For example, academic audiences typically prefer an intellectually based presentation heavy with facts, figures, research, and theory, while a teenage audience, who may also be interested in facts and figures, requires a better balance of intellect, emotion, and entertainment.

3. *Display an understanding attitude.* When audience members express opinions contrary to your content, express an understanding of their comments, then quickly return to your initial arguments. Something like, "Thank you for expressing that point of view. I came to a different conclusion because…" works in any situation.

Conclusion

As a rich dessert signals the end of a delicious meal, the conclusion signals the final message in a presentation. The wrap-up. Effective conclusions are unique in style and approach. They are smooth rather than abrupt. And potent in their content.

Effective conclusions tie together the gist of the core content message with the objectives of the presentation and pave the way for audience members to draw their own natural conclusions, which should be exactly the same as the conclusions you have provided. Effective conclusions are (1) concisely stated, (2) emotionally linked, and (3) require action.

The more memorable conclusions are those that offer something distinctive. For example, when the presentation ends with an opportunity for the audience to hear, see, touch, smell, or feel something related to the core content, the message becomes more memorable. Automobile manufacturers are experts in this tactic. They often have a model of the product for the audience to see, feel, and touch at the conclusion of the presentation. Politicians like to conclude their campaign presentations with loud, upbeat music and balloons filling the air, which is an idea that can be modified to be applicable in any concluding situation. Participation and sensory stimulation make the conclusion more memorable.

Encore

The encore is that final, extra piece of presentation, information, or entertainment that leaves the audience feeling good and wanting more. Every presentation should have an encore step; however, most presenters do not know how to deliver the encore step. Somewhat like the encore at a concert, when the orchestra plays one last, wonderful piece of music, the encore in a presentation is that last story, thought, or piece of information that you leave the audience with. It is the last thought-provoking comment, humorous story, or motivating comment that you give them—literally your last words.

To make a smooth transition from the conclusion to the encore, the presenter must alert the audience that the encore is coming. Some phrases that the presenter can use to alert audience attention to the encore are:

"One last story I'd like to share before I go."
"I'd like to give you one more example before we wind up."
"As you reflect on the messages of today, consider..."

Often the last emotion that the audience experiences is the one that they will associate with the entire experience. Therefore, the nature of the encore should be lighthearted or thought-provoking but not saddening, threatening, or worrisome in any way.

There are three effective encore styles that consistently work well in all audience situations. Use any one of the three techniques alone or in combination with each other to create a memorable presentation.

Effective Encore Presentation Techniques

1. *Weave a common thread.* Tie the objectives and proposed solutions of the presentation to the needs and interests of the audience. Specifically point out common threads that unite your presentation with their values and objectives.

2. *Leave them laughing.* Laughter has a pleasant, positive, and uplifting effect on people. If the final emotion triggered is the one thereafter associated with the entire presentation, you can count on laughter to provide a positive, pleasant emotion that will counteract or balance any unpleasant messages that may have been delivered in the core presentation.

3. *Leave them wanting more.* Too much of a good thing is bad. In all presentations there is a point at which too much begins to wear thin, to become tiresome, boring, redundant, or worn. There comes a point after which more is less. Stop short of this point. Remember, it's nice to be asked to come, but it's even nicer to be asked to come back.

The best intended presentations can quickly and unintentionally be spoiled by thoughtless comments or behavior. Protect your memorable image and well-planned presentation by checking ahead of time for these spoilers:

Presentation Spoilers

1. *Too much "I."* The focus of the presentation is on anything but you, so avoid this first person pronoun.

2. *Inaccuracy.* Check your facts. Inaccurate data immediately destroy credibility and trust, and ultimately your image.

3. *Emotional reactions.* Although you can be passionate about the topic, keep personal emotions and reactions out of your presentation.

4. *Obvious nervousness.* As presenter or host, you are considered the expert in charge and must display confidence. A less than confident appearance equates to a less than successful engagement.

5. *All work and no play.* A lack of balance in your presentation tilts the emotional state of the audience into the pits of deadly seriousness, an emotional void that is less than memorable.

6. *Political incorrectness.* Don't be afraid to disagree with conventional wisdom, but off-color stories, poor grammar usage, and gender or racial biases represent both a lack of sensitivity to your audience and a lack of taste.

5

Emotional Links: A Memory-Making Strategy

*"There are two distinct classes of what are called thoughts;
those that we produce in ourselves by reflection and the act
of thinking, and those that bolt into the mind on their own."*

—*Thomas Paine*

Emotional links are the connectors between an event, activity, or person and the targeted audience. They are the conduits through which outside messages and experiences link up to a person's internal emotions, thus causing some type of reaction to occur.

Think of each emotional link as a personal, outward extension of a closely held emotion in an individual. Like a tentacle dangling from an emotional base, the emotional link acts as a channel through which messages and experiences are processed by an individual. When an outside event or message touches a strong emotional link in a person, a memory-making moment has occurred. But when an event or message touches a weak emotional link, or can find no emotional link to connect to, nothing memorable occurs.

Because people are comprised of a complex set of emotions of various origins and degrees of intensity, the design and description of their emotional links are equally complex. Among this pile of infinitely diverse emotional links there seem to be a number of common links. Targeting a select few of these emotional links will open the gateway to opportunities for creating memorable moments.

Common Personal Emotions and Needs

- Love
- Sadness
- Envy
- Hatred
- Security
- Status

- Fear
- Compassion
- Excitement
- Resentment
- Survival
- Safety

- Happiness
- Caring
- Acceptance
- Righteousness
- Passion
- Achievement

- Anger
- Greed
- Guilt
- Fairness
- Friendship
- Anxiety

Pushing the Right Buttons

The awareness of an individual's emotional profile, in other words, the presence and mix of emotions within, makes that person a more manageable target for creating memory-making moments. The cliché "she knows how to push his buttons" refers to how one person can manipulate another's feelings and actions by saying or doing something that is linked to a particular strong emotion. When you understand the strongest emotions residing within someone, you can directly manage that person's behavior by playing into or away from those emotions in order to generate a desired response. This is not meant to be a negative manipulation but rather a positive approach that serves the interests of both parties.

Emotional profiles are complicated, sophisticated, and difficult to decipher even when one has extensive training. Strong emotional links display themselves repeatedly through various behaviors, word choices, actions, treatment of others, and treatment of the self. One can identify the strong emotional links in another person through observation and experience with them.

To identify the strongest emotional links in an individual, look for common themes or messages in what that person says or does. Focus on the list of commonly held emotions previously provided and monitor the frequency and intensity of each emotion you observe in the other person. Strong themes will quickly emerge. These themes represent the dominant or strongest emotions of the person at the time of observation. They are the emotions most vulnerable to memory-making opportunities. They are the emotions upon which memorable relationships and events can be built.

Relationships of Commonly Held Emotional Links

The probability of creating a memorable event or image is greatest when the strongest emotions or needs in a person are actively recognized, supported, and nurtured. For example, consider a compassionate person, one who possesses a deep feeling of sympathy for others stricken by misfortune. Events that touch an emotional link that is connected to the compassion emotion in this person will be memorable. The stronger the emotional link for compassion is, the more memorable the event will be. For example, the discovery of an injured animal would trigger compassionate people to feel deep sympathy for the animal. It is the emotional link triggered by the discovery of the needy animal that will make this event memorable to a compassionate person.

Consistency

Consistency in behavior represents a solidly connected emotional link, a conduit that is anchored at one end in an emotion and at the other end in a set of consistent behaviors. The fundamental nature of these consistent behaviors, regardless of their scope or significance, provides a sense of security and predictability that adds to their memory-making characteristics.

For example, every year for the past twenty years, Frank, Sr. and Frank, Jr., father and son, have made it a point to watch the Sunday football game together. If they can't be in the same location to watch the game together, then they watch it in their respective locations and connect for conversation over the telephone! Without a miss, Frank, Jr. will call Frank, Sr. after the first play of the game, and they will talk on the telephone through the entire game, just as if they were sitting side by side. It is not the team or the game that is memorable in this situation. It is the consistent behavior of being together at a predetermined time and place for a predetermined purpose, a predictable behavior that is memorable.

Consistent behaviors can create memorably favorable or unfavorable images, which are thereafter difficult to change. They can boost or bury your personal or professional life. For example, consistently tardy, grumpy, or noncooperative behaviors are unfavorable qualities that are difficult to forget, and therefore difficult to overcome once they have been consistently displayed.

If you wish to transform consistent behaviors into memorable behaviors, use the following five-step process as an action plan.

1. *Conduct a self-evaluation.* Choose the target audience you want to make yourself memorable to. List behaviors and qualities they view as desirable, and then those qualities they view as undesirable. Which of your behaviors and qualities are on each list?

2. *Neutralize negatives.* Highlight undesirable behaviors that you currently have and plan to substitute desirable behaviors for the undesirable ones. Choose the top three to five undesirable behaviors and make immediate changes.

3. *Accentuate positives.* Review the list of qualities and behaviors your targeted audience finds desirable. Choose three to five new, desirable behaviors or qualities and add them to your repertoire of behaviors.

4. *Match emotional links.* Identify the strong emotional links in your audience. Match your desirable behaviors to the strongest emotional links. You should have multiple desirable behaviors matched to each of the strong emotional links in your audience. The more desirable behaviors you have feeding each strong emotional link, the more likely you are to be memorable to that audience.

5. *Build on consistency.* Identify a number of desirable behaviors that can be transformed into traditions of consistent behavior. The frequency of the tradition is not as important as the fact that it is a defined experience, or consistent behavior. Consistency is the primary element that makes a tradition a tradition—an activity that is repeatedly engaged in given a certain set of circumstances or timings.

Emotional Holes and Emotional Wholes

Life has a way of kicking people around. Disappointments, empty dreams, unfulfilled needs, and hurt feelings are on the short list of experiences all people have had at one time or another. Everyone has had some share of emotional pain or disappointment. Learning the nature of emotional holes, or voids, in another person allows you to plan events, create experiences, and modify behaviors to soothe the pain and unleash a range of positive, memorable feelings. Uncovering the emotional holes is the challenge. Often they are so deeply buried that only pieces are evident.

Because emotional holes in adults have generally existed for a long period of time, filling the void will bring a strong emotional response. Here's a case in point. Two sets of golf clubs and accessories were purchased as gifts for two different people. One set was given to a budding teenage golfer. He was genuinely pleased, responding with many thanks and hugs. Clearly he was appreciative, but it probably was not a memorable event for him.

The second set of golf clubs was given to the teenager's grandfather, a lifelong golfer who had played with a set of odds and ends, makeshift clubs, for thirty years. When the grandfather saw his gift of a set of shining Calloway clubs and accessories, tears welled in his eyes. It was a memory-making moment for him. Somehow an emotional void was filled, the legacy of an earlier life of much deprivation.

To uncover emotional voids and sensitivities, listen to what other people tell you about themselves as they explain their life and feelings. Focus on what they say with respect to:

1. How *important* they feel in the lives of those they love.
2. How *loved* they feel by those who are important to them.
3. How *involved* they feel with those who are important to them.
4. How *secure* they feel about their future.
5. What unfulfilled dreams and wishes they have held for a long time.

These are the typical areas within which emotional holes are likely to be found.

Building on Emotional Links

To build a memorable event or image with the help of emotional links, follow these four steps:

1. *Identify* the strong emotional links of your targeted audience.
2. *Applaud* these qualities.
3. *Create,* discover, or engineer many events that will closely connect with the strong emotional links of the targeted audience.
4. *Reinforce* to the targeted audience the correlation between their experiences and strong emotional links and yourself as the change agent.

Emotional Links in a Business Situation

If we think of a business as a living entity with a personality, values, and objectives, then it is easy to conceive of a business as possessing emotional links. Emotional links used to develop personal relationships are different from emotional links used to develop business relationships. Business relationships are often made memorable by linking up to actions and behaviors that are related to one or more of the following common corporate emotional links.

- Caring
- Leadership
- Security
- Team spirit
- Quality
- Market share
- Competition
- Survival
- Vision
- Professionalism
- Innovation
- Integrity
- Strength
- Dominance
- Brotherhood
- Economics
- Customer satisfaction
- Organizational growth

The exact profile of organizational emotional links will vary greatly from one entity to another, and they will be interpreted differently from leader to leader and from boss to boss within each entity. Tying your behavior and actions to the organization's strong emotional links will make you fit in, yet stand out above the crowd. However, tying your behavior to weak corporate emotional links will be a career killer because you can then be viewed as a mismatch with the organization's profile or direction.

Determining Emotional Links in Your Business or Career

How are the strong emotional links possessed by your employer, or would-be employer, identified? Observation and research are the keys. Observe your boss, your boss's boss, and the organization's president. Listen to the kinds of words they use. Listen to the goals they speak of. Certain themes and descriptive words will emerge in a pattern of presentations, speeches, memos, goal statements, company correspondence, and communications. Identify those themes. Frequency of mention is one indicator of the intensity of an emotional link. Frequent mentions could indicate the strength of an emotional link and therefore its importance to the organization.

Research the recent past and the culture of the organization. Obvious emotional links from the recent past may provide insight into current emotional links. What was valued or important to an organizational entity rarely changes rapidly. Talk to leaders in the organization. What themes do they see and hear frequently now? What themes were dominant in recent years?

To build your memorable image in the hallowed halls of corporate America, follow these steps:

1. *Identify* the top business initiatives and the strong emotional links for your targeted organization, as well as the top executives involved with these emotional links and initiatives.

2. *Applaud* the emotional links identified and their importance to the organization through frequent references to them.

3. *Brainstorm* how your position, talents, and even unknown skills could be developed to interface with, add value to, or support and assist the efforts of these top executives. Think creatively. Avoid obvious or mundane approaches. The interface can be an extensive ongoing relationship, or it can be an initial onetime event. If it is a onetime event, the approach must be very bold—extreme, unexpected in style and substance—to make it stand out.

4. *Engineer* opportunities to play the roles outlined above. This may take some ingenuity. Be creative and imaginative.

5. *Be bold.* Be confident. Be passionate. Be persistent. Don't look back. Many people get to this point but cannot gather enough boldness or confidence to go forward. Make yourself memorable and go forward.

The M Factors: Memory-Making Boosters

Memory-making boosters serve the purpose of defining and explaining an effective approach to making yourself memorable. They serve to organize approaches to creating a memorable image or event, but they do not create the memorable status until they are joined by one or more of the distinguishing memory-making factors, called M factors (see Figure 5-1).

There are shadings or variations to each of the M factors. Understanding the principle behind each factor will direct your efforts in preparing a personal strategy to make you memorable. Think of these factors in broad, general terms, keeping the big picture in mind. Use the specific illustrations provided to communicate what is intended by each factor and how it works, but don't limit your thinking to that alone. Take each factor and think of ways to apply it to your situation to create a memorable image or event.

Figure 5-1 Memory-making M factors.

- **EXTREMES**
- **FIRSTS**
- **BESTS**
- **CONTRARIANISM**
- **LEADERSHIP**
- **SHARING**

The M Factor: Extremes

Extremes are one-of-a-kind experiences that represent the far-thest end of the experience spectrum: either the best or the worst of a particular type of experience. Because they are unique by virtue of their definition, extremes have the potential to become memorable when the situation, circumstance, or event is emo-tionally linked. Examples of extremes that most people can identify with are:

- The hottest summer
- The saddest moment
- The worst boss
- The scariest situation
- The most serious mistake

- The worst storm
- The happiest moment
- The greatest success
- The most generous person
- The grimmest situation

Extremes that the audiences approve of, or believe to be true, are more memorable than extremes they do not approve of, or do not believe to be true.* For example, if audience members are told that you are the best boss they will ever have, and they happen to believe that this is true, then it is likely that you will be memorable to that audience as the best boss they ever had. On the other hand, if the audience is told that you are the best boss they will ever have, but they don't believe this to be so, you will never be remembered by this audience as the best boss they ever had. Extremes and believability are a potent combination.

Building on Extremes

The key to building on extremes is to identify the strong emo-tional links in the audience. Without this information, the tactic of extremes will be fruitless, as it will not become memorable. With this information, the tactic of extremes is a potent memory maker.

Five easy steps to building a memorable image or event using extremes are as follows:

---

*Marvin Karlins and Herbert Abelson, *Persuasion*, 2nd ed. (New York: Springer Publishing Company, 1970), p. 24.

1. *Identify* the strongest emotional links residing in the target audience.
2. *Applaud* these strong emotional links.
3. *Engineer* a positive experience based on one or more of the strongest emotional links.
4. *Build* at least one extreme element into the experience engineered.
5. *Reinforce* the extreme descriptive elements to the target audience as the experience is occurring. Then, reinforce the uniqueness or extreme nature of the total experience at the conclusion of the experience, recounting to the audience how the extreme elements of the experience tie into the overall positive experience they are having. This will emotionally link the audience to the event and to you.

For example, you want to send your spouse a message of affection. A bouquet of flowers would initially seem like a good idea—not particularly unique or memorable, but a good idea. If the M factor "extremes" is used, the resulting memorable event might look something like the following situation—a campaign.

Day one—morning:	A short personal note from you arrives at your wife's office. Enclosed in the note is a pressed flower from the garden and a short poetic message of love.
Day one—afternoon:	A large bouquet of flowers arrives at the office with a second poetic message of love. The bouquet is very impressive. It is a public display of affection, seen by all your wife's co-workers. The more dramatic the display, the greater the gossip will be, a bonus for you in the overall effort to create a memorable experience.
Day two—morning:	A small gift box is delivered to your wife's office. Wrapped in floral motif gift wrap, the enclosed gift is a silk scarf painted in floral designs.

	The note says, "I wanted to give you flowers. Please accept the everlasting artistic flowers of this gift."
Day two—evening:	Arriving for dinner at home, you pick from the garden a bouquet of flowers for the dinner table or bedside stand.
Day three—afternoon:	You send a message to your wife inviting her to meet you in the yard of your residence, where a special surprise awaits. You meet in the yard as planned. Greeting her with a glass of wine, you usher her to a nearby newly planted flower garden lined in ribbon. Walking her to the middle of the garden, you point to the engraved stone with her name on it. A unique way of presenting the unique gift of a garden.

In this example, it is the extreme number of days and ways in which the message of love was delivered. No one aspect of the giving was especially memorable in and of itself. It is the wholeness of the experience, the combination of multiple facets of extremes that provides the memorable quality. The pattern of extremes in this example could theoretically extend endlessly, or as long as your creativity and wallet permit. However, there is a point at which the law of diminishing returns sets in, novelty wears thin, and the effort begins to lose its pizzazz. Know when to stop.

The M Factor: Bests

"If you would be remembered, do one thing superbly well," says Saunder Norvell. To be "best" means to be better than the rest. It is a matter of positioning. And that positioning gives it a memory-making quality. Slightly better, or moderately better than the rest, is not distinctive enough to make it memorable. To be memorable it must be significantly better—it must be best.

"Best" can also be an individual, relative judgment of quality personally ascribed to someone or something. The "best" person, place, or thing, in this sense, does not necessarily become memorable. A "best" is more likely to become memorable when it is emotionally linked.

The following are examples of "bests":

- Best friend
- Best dress
- Best value
- Best job
- Best decision
- Best idea
- Best results
- Best investment
- Best experience

To make something memorable based on the tactic of its being "best" requires identification of the strong emotional links in the targeted audience and the creation of a "best" experience that relates to that emotional link.

The M Factor: Firsts

"Nobody remembers who came in second," said Charles Schultz. First-time events, like first-place winners, often become memorable. It is of the nature of firsts to be memorable. However, not all first events become memorable. What distinguishes a memorable "first" event or person from a non-memorable one?

Memorable first-time events are generally emotionally linked or unexpected in nature. Common emotions associated with first-time events include fear, anxiety, and anticipation.

For example, the first roller coaster ride is both a first experience and a strong emotionally linked experience heightened by anticipation and anxiety. Once the first roller coaster ride is over, subsequent rides may be thrilling, but none will be as memorable or as whole as the first ride experience.

Memorable First Experiences

Once a memorable first experience has been created, it will remain memorable thereafter, never being unseated by a future event of the same kind, but enrolled always in the exclusive company of other memorable firsts. There are numerous common,

emotionally linked career and life experiences that would qualify
as memorable firsts for many people. For example:

- Your first job
- Your first promotion
- Your first marriage
- Your first apartment
- Your first boss
- The first time you were fired
- Your first baby
- Your first hospital experience
- Your first teacher
- Your first school

These are illustrative of the principle of firsts. Whether or
not the specific examples selected are memorable for you, you
can use them to shape your thinking about the value of first
experiences and events.

To use the factor of firsts to create a memorable experience
or image, follow these four steps:

1. *Identify* strong emotional links in the targeted audience.
2. *Applaud* the strong emotional links.
3. *Discover*, create, or engineer a first experience that relates
   to one of the strong emotional links possessed by the
   audience.
4. *Participate* in the "first" experience with the audience.
   Participation is essential for associating your image with
   the memorable state of this "first" event.

The more extreme the "first" experience is, and the more
closely it is associated with one or more strong emotional links,
the more likely it is that the event, and you as its sponsor, will
become memorable.

The M Factor: Contrarianism

Contrarianism is a unique way of thinking and doing that is
characterized by taking an approach that runs contrary to popular belief and behavior. For example, when the stock market is
plummeting and the majority of investors are selling, the contrarian investor is buying. Or when popular public opinion
looks unfavorably upon a situation, the contrary view is to find

some redeeming value in it. Whatever the masses are doing, the contrarian is looking to do the opposite.

Contrarianism has the potential to make you memorable because it causes you to stand apart from the crowd. A strategic use of a contrarian approach with an emotionally linked circumstance could prove to be extremely memorable. Take this hypothetical example: The board of trustees of a prominent corporation is planning to cut jobs and expenses to meet its profit goals. The contrarian thinker disapproves of this course, voicing his objections to worker cutbacks, and viewing the challenge to be one of increasing productivity rather than of reducing the work force. Crowds of workers rally around the contrarian, pledging to follow his direction in the contrarian approach, which will save their jobs. This is the emotional link that makes the contrarian's behavior memorable.

Execution of a wisely thought-out contrarian approach is essential to the success of the factor. Unlike the factors of firsts, bests, or emotional links, the contrarian factor usually allows for only one pass at the effort. The cynics and naysayers, who are a part of the majority of common thinkers, are waiting to see the contrarian approach fail, at which time the "I told you so" people will be unlikely to permit a second or third effort at execution. Brave contrarian thinkers become memorable in the minds of others at the point when the powerful results of uncommon, contrarian thinking are successful.

Use the following four steps to prepare a contrarian approach

1. *Define the problem.* Make no assumptions that you know what it is until you have fully defined it.

2. *Outline options.* Brainstorm. Avoid obvious solutions. Focus on solutions that go contrary to common thinking.

3. *Select a solution.* Choose a solution that is different from what common, mass thinking would dictate should be done. Test the contrarian factor by asking, "How different is this approach from that which common thinking would choose?" If the answer is "significantly different," then you may have a good solution.

4. *Test the selected option.* Ask the questions, "If we were to adopt the contrary solution, what would be the worst thing that could happen? What would be the best thing that could happen?" If the best possible thing that could happen is superior to, or more powerful than, the worst possible thing that could happen, support the contrarian approach.

Be aware that an overuse of contrarianism can be misunderstood and possibly result in your acquiring a reputation for being difficult or a misfit. Contrarianism is not naysaying or obstructionism.

The M Factor: Sharing

Sharing is defined as parceling out, or doling out, a portion of something to another. Literally, anything can be "shared" in some way. For example:

- Material goods
- Information
- Knowledge
- Thoughts

Of the seven M factors used to distinguish and boost the impact of emotional links, sharing is the only factor requiring the involvement of another person to complete the act. One cannot share alone. You can create firsts or bests and carry out each of the other six factors without the involvement of another person, but sharing is a tactic that requires the participation of the targeted audience in the form of its being receptive to the shared gift.

Sharing becomes memorable when what is shared is highly valued by the receiver. The more value the shared item holds, the more memorable it will become.

When Does the Sharing Factor Make You Memorable?

The sharing factor is most effective in either one or both of the following situations:

1. *It makes the other person feel important.* On an individual or professional level, sharing is a personal experience. The

more important the other person is made to feel via the sharing experience, the more likely it is that the experience will be memorable.

2. *The price of sharing is high.* There are two parties in a sharing situation—the "giver" and the "getter." When the giver puts himself at risk by sharing, the cost of sharing is high. The higher the risk and the higher the price, the more memorable the sharing experience will likely be. For example, if food rations are low, hunger is high, and the sharing of food occurs, the cost of that sharing is high, even life-threatening, and therefore the memorable impact of that experience will also be high.

The M Factor: Leadership

Leadership is the ability to get others to follow you. This implies moving ahead, making progress. Many people attempt, formally, to lead, but few actually succeed. Only those who succeed become memorable.

People want to be led, particularly in times of crisis or in circumstances unfamiliar or frightening to them. These situations are ripe for creating a memorable image—even a heroic image.

Franklin D. Roosevelt used leadership to bring the United States through the Great Depression and into World War II. When uncertainty among Americans was high and jobs were scarce, when a national financial crisis was at hand and no one had answers, FDR's resolution, inspiration, and willingness to experiment made him memorable to all those who benefited from his leadership.

Leadership, as a strategy for creating a memorable image, is effective only when the results of leadership provide a significant and valued benefit to the followers. Results that are not valued are viewed as ineffective leadership, a failed or muted attempt at best.

When Leadership Will Make You Memorable

Not all circumstances lend themselves to leadership as an effective M factor. There are, however, four sets of circumstances in which the leadership factor will be extremely effective in making you memorable. Take the lead when:

- You can do what others cannot.
- Followers elect you to lead.
- There is a crisis.
- Alternative leaders are less capable than you.

Leadership suggests goal setting, progress, confidence, power, and success. Because there are few true leaders, those who become so are held in the highest regard. Because true leadership is a rare commodity, those who have it are heroes of a sort.

Leadership by Lee Iacocca, former CEO of the Chrysler Corporation, caused him to be viewed as a hero by many workers who otherwise would have lost their jobs had the downward decline of the organization not been reversed. Companies or careers in crisis, saved through leadership and restored to good health, view the leader as a hero.

Leadership, as a memory-making factor, can be achieved on any scale and with any size audience. You can be a leader to children, to other adults, to anyone, in fact, who wants you to lead and is content to follow.

When the results of the leadership effort are emotionally linked to the audience, the leader and the event become memorable. The stronger the emotional link is, the more memorable the event and leader will be.

6

Unexpected Incidents: A Memory-Making Strategy

"Never make forecasts, especially about the future."
—*Samuel Goldwyn*

Many unexpected incidents occur daily and frequently go unnoticed, never to be recalled again. They are routine in and of themselves. However, occasionally, unexpected incidents become memorable. Northwestern upsets Notre Dame University in a seasonal football game, September 2, 1995. Your boss gives you a $500 bonus for finishing a project earlier than expected. And Scrooge has a change of heart, generously sharing with Tiny Tim's family. These are examples of unexpected events that became memorable. What makes one unexpected incident memorable, and another not?

Consider two illness situations: a life-threatening event, and the onslaught of a common cold. When a person is unexpectedly taken ill with a common cold, the intensity of the experience is low. Although unexpected in nature, it is something that we have some familiarity and past experience with. We know what to expect in terms of the impact on our life; thus the probability of the event becoming memorable is low. However, if a person is unexpectedly taken ill with a life-threatening disease, the outcome and impact of the event are quite unknown; thus the intensity of the experience is much higher, and the probability that this event will become memorable is greater.

Both situations involve an unexpected illness, yet one is memorable and the other is not. Where do the differences lie?

In this case, the differences between the two unexpected incidents are in three areas representing two different M factors:

1. The strength of intensity of the life-threatening situation compared to the lower intensity of the common cold event (extremes).
2. The lack of familiarity with the life-threatening experience (firsts).
3. The seriousness of the situation's potential implications (extremes).

Unexpected incidents alone cannot create a memorable event without the assistance of one or more M factors, which act as tactical boosters to the strategy. As you will recall from Chapter 5, the six M factors are extremes, firsts, bests, contrarianism, leadership, and sharing. The more M factors that are associated with an incident, the more memorable the event is likely to be. Think of the unexpected incident as a strategy for making yourself memorable, and the tactical boosters as the distinguishing elements that separate one incident from another, making one more memorable.

A surprise birthday party, for example, is unexpected by definition, but not necessarily memorable. Surprise birthday parties that do become memorable do so in spite of the element of "surprise." They become memorable because of the existence of M factors associated with the event.

Continuing with the example of a surprise birthday party, and adding M factor elements, a truly memorable event can be planned. Consider the following M factors as ideas for either a surprise birthday party or the next celebratory event you will direct.

M Factors for a Surprise Birthday Event

Extremes:
- Largest cake
- Largest guest list
- Most extensive display of food
- Most extensive display of decorations
- South Seas theme—something unusual
- Guests in native South Seas costumes

	• A "pirates" clan hired to kidnap the guest of honor
Firsts:	• Location on a floating barge
	• First-time event, never before done
	• Tons of sand imported to the deck of the barge to transform it into a beach
Bests	• Best chef employed for food preparation
	• Best band to provide entertainment
	• Best champagne used for the toasts

Note: Three M factors are applicable here. Not all M factors are applicable in all situations.

Career/Professional Examples

The same set of memory-making characteristics is as effective in professional arenas as personal arenas. What makes one job candidate more memorable than others? One sales representative more memorable than another? Or one advertising campaign more memorable than another? The answer lies in the individual's ability to creatively employ one or more M factors in concert with an unexpected event.

For example, one sales rep successfully lands a desired account by creatively gaining the targeted audience's attention via unexpected events. This is how it happened.

The targeted audience is a physician's office staff. Marcia, the pharmaceutical sales rep, needs an appointment with the doctor in order to present the new drug line. But the physician's staff has been directed to make no appointments with sales reps. Marcia works around the situation by making herself memorable, and in turn gains access to an appointment with the physician. First, she tries the conventional approach. She introduces herself, the company she represents, and the product line. Cut off in mid-sentence by the office staff, Marcia changes strategies, continuing to talk with staff members, but on a personal, social level, breaking down barriers and finding common links, such as work challenges, personal interests, or family events, to talk about. Unsuccessful in getting an appointment, she leaves on a friendly acquaintance basis.

The following day, Marcia forwards a gift to the office staff. The gift is a goldfish in a bowl. The fish is named Max, a personal touch. On each of the next four days, another goldfish arrives. At the end of the week, Marcia calls upon the office staff, again asking for an appointment. The goldfish experience provides her entrée to a barrier-free conversation. The office staff has had so much fun with the goldfish incident that they persuade the physician to make an exception and meet Marcia.

In this situation, Marcia made herself memorable by using an unexpected incident laced with a few M factors. The unexpected incident was the receipt of a gift by the office staff. The M factors were:

Extremes: • The number of gifts that were given: five
                 • The number of days over which the gift giving extended: five

Firsts: • First time the office staff had heard of, or seen, a fish given as a gift
                 • First time they had experienced such moxie and imaginative flair in a sales rep

Always Desired, but Never Acquired

My mother once said, "When you stop wanting things, you're dead." In many ways this is true. People seem to have an eternal desire for "things." Some of the things we desire are current items—things we see at the shopping mall, on television, or at a friend's house.

Other desired things are from years gone by—things we always desired, but somehow never acquired. They remain highly desirable in the archives of our heart. The reason for their "never acquired" status may be the economics of the time, or it may be some greater emotional connection to the past. The reason is not so important. What is important is that it was highly desired and has remained so over the years.

Consider the story of one of my adult friends. Growing up in a working-class environment forty years ago, he thought that the greatest thing of all would be to own a cigar box filled with dimes. As a child, that dream was never fulfilled. Now, fast forward forty years, and he has become a successful businessman. He tells the story of wanting a dime-filled cigar box—something he could easily do for himself now, but never has.

Wanting to make myself memorable, I knew just what to do. On his next birthday, I presented him with that long-coveted dime-filled cigar box! Actually, it was more than that. It was the fulfillment of a lifelong desire, a memorable event for him—the attainment of an "always desired, but never acquired" item. Who would think that a dime-filled cigar box could represent so much!

Exploring "always desired" files of a person's mind is likely to bring forth some interesting ideas as to how you can make yourself memorable to that person. Sort out the ideas that are emotionally linked from those that are simply material desires. Fulfillment of emotionally linked desires has a greater probability of making you memorable.

Routine Events Made Memorable

How does one take a routine daily event and make it memorable? Routine events become memorable when something unexpected affects the routine. Because so much of life is routine, opportunities for creating unexpected events are plentiful. One of the easiest ways to turn a routine event into a memorable, unexpected event is to radically change one or more of the key situational elements. Key elements are defined as the answers to the questions: who, what, when, where, why, or how. The more elements that are changed, the more memorable the event is likely to be.

"Who" addresses the people involved in the situation. Changing this element means changing the people routinely involved. The element of "what" describes the actual event that is occurring. "When" defines the usual timing for the event. "Where" describes the location in which the event routinely occurs. "Why" tells the purpose behind the routine activity, and "how" informs us of the means by which the event is carried out. Let's use a routine staff meeting as an example.

Routine Elements	*Unexpected Changes*
Who:	Change attendees. Invite customers and others you would not normally include. Include a "first."
What:	Change agenda items. Critique the purpose of the meeting and adjust it accordingly. Include a "first."
Where:	Change the meeting location. Make it poolside or in the local park. Be creative. Include a "first."
When:	Schedule it for an unusual time, for example, 6:00 A.M. Include a "first."
How:	Dramatically change the way the meeting is organized and how it is managed. Call for more or less participation than is usual, greater or fewer activities. Change the roles of meeting attendees. Create a "first."

Add M factor elements whenever you change a routine function. The M factor of "first" is one that has many applications in routine functions. The more M factor applications there are in an event, the more memorable it will be. If the unexpected event in routine behaviors does not involve M factors, it will be just a passing event, quite unmemorable.

It is tradition at our house for my father to carve the Thanksgiving turkey. Meat carving is a time-honored privilege of the head of the household. Last year, as the carving set was presented to Dad, he ceremoniously passed it to his son with instructions that he "learn to carve the turkey"—essentially, and unexpectedly, changing the "who" in this previously routine holiday tradition, and adding the M factor of "first." For members of the family, it was a memorable event as the passing of a tradition occurred. For my brother, it represented the first time he was asked to conduct this time-honored tradition. As a holiday, it would be more memorable than others.

In a work environment, you can use unexpected events to make yourself memorable. Here's what one CEO of a hospital did when he wanted to reward a small group of managers who had worked hard on an important and complex project. Past recognitions would have been a pat on the back, a plaque for their wall, or lunch with the boss. This time the CEO wanted to make a statement, to make himself and the event memorable. So, to the surprise and astonishment of everyone, the CEO awarded each team member a round trip ticket for two to the Caribbean! They were in shock! What made this event memorable? M factors contributing to making this event memorable were:

- The "extreme" generosity of the gift. The cost of the award was substantially more than the CEO had ever given before.
- This was the "first" time anything of this nature had been given as a recognition.
- The award was somewhat "contrary" to what conventional health care executives would think of doing.
- It was unexpected.

Was the event memorable? Yes. Did the CEO make himself memorable? Definitely.

Unexpected Personalized Events

One direct route to creating a memorable image or event is through unexpected personalization. Arrange as many of the routine elements of who, what, when, where, why, or how an event operates to personalize it for the targeted audience, and assuredly there will be an emotional link strong enough to make it memorable.

For example, the Four Seasons Hotel created a number of unexpected personal incidents that caused my stay there to stand out as one of the most memorable hotel experiences I've ever had. Stepping up to the registration desk at the hotel, I was greeted by the typically friendly hotel staff. Once I gave my name, a stream of unexpected incidents began to occur. The desk clerk told me that the Four Seasons had noticed that on my last stay in one of its hotels, which was not in the same city, I had asked for extra towels and an iron and ironing board, had drunk several bottles of sparkling water and select fruit juices from the mini bar, used the laundry service, and stayed in a nonsmoking room with a view on an upper level. Amazing! They knew so much about me. What made the event memorable was not the surprise of the extraordinary amount of personal information they had gathered from my last visit, but the way in which they used that information to create an unusual personalized experience.

The hotel had taken the liberty of stocking my room with extra towels, an iron and ironing board, and several bottles of sparkling water and select fruit juices in the mini bar, and assigned me a nonsmoking room on the upper level with a view—all without request. The staff created an unexpected personalized experience which made it memorable enough to end up in this book! (M factors of extremes, firsts, and bests applied.)

Four little words sum up what lifted this hotel provider above all others—*a little bit more*. They did all that was expected and a little bit more—the unexpected.

Subsequent to this experience, I've learned that the management of the Four Seasons Hotel has made it a business priority to catalog and manage customer profiles. No wonder so many five-star hotels belong to this one organization. They know how to create memorable unexpected personalized experiences!

If you take these same principles and apply them to a home and family environment, you can make a routine guest visit a memorable event using the following two-step process.

1. *Make a list of the various routine events your guests will experience.* In this case, routine experiences include meals, recreational television, idle conversations, shopping, and general relaxation.

2. *For each routine experience, list ideas that would make the event special and personalized for your guests.* In the case of meals, this might include:

- Preparing their favorite foods
- Specialties and drinks they can get nowhere else
- A dining table with flowers representing their birth month, anniversary, or other special time
- A special welcoming toast to start the meal
- Remembering the guests in the mealtime prayer
- Dinner conversation centering on the guests

- Notable stories of their history and life experiences
- Presentation of a small token gift to each guest

Review your list of ways to personalize the event. Select those events that offer the greatest number, or volume, of ways in which you can personalize the experience. This utilizes the M factor of "extremes" in that the number of personalized events will be greater, or more extreme, than the guest has encountered in the past. Be sure to include any personalized ideas that represent the M factor of "firsts," such as a "first" experience or possession.

The unexpected personalized approach is also effective in making yourself memorable to your boss. Using this strategy, an executive assistant of a client organization, knowing that his boss was interested in maintaining a regular physical fitness schedule, personalized the hotel room where the boss was staying while traveling on business. The personalization included arranging for a stationary bicycle to be put in the room as well as stocking the room with juices and health food snacks. The local athletic club information was obtained and put in his travel file for easy reference. This was not a request made by the boss, but was initiated by the associate in an effort to create a personalized unexpected event through which he hoped to make himself memorable.

Part Three

The Science of Persuasion: Making It Work for You

"We are all salesmen every day of our lives. We are selling our ideas, our plans, our enthusiasm, to those with whom we come into contact."

—Charles Schwab

Persuasion is a combination of science and artistic application. Science represents the projection of normally expected behaviors and results, given specific situations.

For example, research tell us that arguments presented at the beginning or end of a communication generally are better remembered than arguments presented in the middle. To make this information work for you, choose to position your most important arguments either first or last in the communications you send. Other research-based behavioral information that bears on the effectiveness of communication efforts can be used similarly in planning each of your major communication initiatives.

Artistic application is the manner in which an argument is presented and the techniques used to communicate messages and persuade the intended audience. A handful of persuasion techniques, appropriately applied, will effectively manage most situations.

The key to successful persuasion and communication is an understanding of the dynamics of the targeted audience and the matching of the most effective techniques to the dynamics of that audience. In this section we will explore the scientific facts of persuasion and the various techniques or applications of those facts to create an effective, memorable persuasive effort.

7

Persuasion Management

"Men are not influenced by things, but by their thoughts about things."

—*Epictetus*

The act of persuasion is as old as mankind. The story of Eve persuading Adam to eat the forbidden apple in the Garden of Eden is the first recorded act of persuasion. From that day on, we have been using our persuasive skills to make decisions and formulate opinions. Everybody is selling something, using persuasive techniques to communicate ideas, opinions, or recommendations regarding their wares. Understanding the effective elements of persuasion positions you strategically to prepare your campaign or argument with the highest probability of success. As one very successful leader noted: Everything has to be sold.

Research tells us that individual and group behavior can often be influenced. Understanding the art and elements of persuasion and influence allow you to manage the circumstances and produce the most desirable outcomes possible. Often, it is through effective persuasive situations that one becomes memorable. For example, if the results of your persuasive effort result in the approval of an innovative product or process, you will become memorable by association with that innovation. The ability to persuade is a primary tool or skill that helps position you to be memorable.

Nothing happens by accident. The sequence of events and the interrelationships of various factors influence one another and the final outcome. A knowledge and understanding of the influencing factors and how they work is an advantage in preparing, positioning, and delivering your persuasive argument.

The following eight influencing factors are largely responsible for the outcomes of persuasive efforts. Knowledge of their interrelationships and of their impact on the audience allows you to intelligently pick and choose the components of your presentation on the basis of the audience profile so as to maximize the desired outcome.

1. Timing
2. Use of logic or emotion
3. Credibility
4. Positive or negative spin
5. Persuadability
6. Having more than one position
7. Durability of effects of persuasive techniques
8. Profile of the effective persuader

Timing Is Everything

The success or failure of a persuasive effort is often directly tied to the timing of the effort. Today's unacceptable idea could be tomorrow's grand success story.

For every concept there is a limited window of opportunity or receptivity. Sometimes that window of opportunity is clearly defined; at others it is ambiguous. When the window of opportunity has closed, the probability of successfully persuading is lessened, so timing your argument is critical.

There are a number of factors that contribute to optimal timing:

1. *Whether other priorities are pushing for audience attention.* It is normal to assume that there will be multiple issues bidding for the audience's time and attention, and that a certain number of issues can be managed simultaneously. But beyond this "certain number," adequate time and attention cannot be paid. The challenge is to position your issue high on the list of priorities, in balance with other pressing issues, but not dominated by them. If this is not possible, then reschedule your effort to a time when your topic will be considered a higher priority.

2. *The level of interest the audience has in the topic presented.* The greater the level of interest in your concern, the higher you will be on the priority list of time, attention, resources, and cooperation. If the audience is distracted by other pressing issues, or has a low degree of interest in your topic to begin with, the most persuasive moments will be the early ones. In this situation, your best and strongest arguments should be positioned early in the presentation in order to receive immediate audience feedback and to avoid allowing your audience to become bored.

3. *The level of focus the audience has on your presentation.* Timing the delivery of your presentation is vital to its survival. Research indicates that arguments presented at the beginning or end of a communication tend to be remembered more easily than arguments presented in the middle.* This information suggests that there is no strategically acceptable position for your presentation but the first or last position. And that it may even be wiser to postpone or reschedule your presentation to a time when it can be positioned first or last rather than risk weakening it by being sandwiched in between.

4. *Other significant incidents occurring around this decision.* For example, any rewarding or punishing incidents that occur close in time to a persuasive argument will influence the thinking of the audience. Incidents perceived as rewarding or satisfying will act as corroborators of your argument and will tend to influence the audience's decision in the direction of your argument. By the same token, punishing or unfavorable incidents that occur close in time to the argument tend to influence the audience's opinion in the direction opposite to your argument.**

This information suggests that the management of incidents surrounding the window of opportunity is critical to the desired outcome. In other words, planning and controlling the persuasive argument means planning and controlling the incidents that are in close time proximity to your persuasive effort.

5. *Environmental factors of the presentation site.* Surprisingly, environmental conditions such as weather, room temperature,

---

* Marvin Karlins and Herbert Abelson, *Persuasion,* 2nd ed. (New York: Springer Publishing Company, 1970), p. 31.
** Ibid., p. 29

and the time of day, week, or month also play a significant role in managing the probability of successful persuasion. Elmer Wheeler's classic book, *How to Put Yourself Across*, details the relationship of weather conditions to decision making. Warm, muggy air or high humidity tend to slow down the speed of the audience, making people slower to respond and less able to focus their attention. By contrast, crisp, cool, sunny, and cheerful days provide environmental support for more rapid decision making and thinking.* Managing the environmental variables as closely as possible may offset what otherwise might be working against your persuasive effort.

In addition to the time of day and type of weather, the physical environment in which the presentation takes place is also an influencer. Larger, more spacious meeting rooms with windows to the outdoors and natural lighting seem to help people to "think bigger," more expansively and creatively, while smaller rooms with harsh artificial lighting confine the scope of creative or possibility thinking, making it more difficult to achieve the desired audience impact.

Logic or Emotion?

Some persuasive approaches are clearly and logically presented, based on a sequence of facts, figures, and conclusions. Other persuasive approaches are bursting with emotionalism. By nature, people are both logical and emotional. The proper choice between a logical presentation and the use of emotionalism depends on the type of audience and decision maker to be influenced.

Some audiences prefer logical presentations, while others are more open to emotional messages. Most people require a blend of both logic and emotion. The art is to know when and how to mix the ingredients. Intelligent audiences require an approach quite different from what less intelligent audiences prefer. And creative people require an approach that differs from what would suit concrete, noncreative thinkers.

Logic has the ability to sway highly intelligent people, who would be turned off by emotional appeals. However, logic can

---

*Ibid., p. 199.

have a baffling effect on less educated people, who seem more vulnerable to emotional appeals commonly grounded in unsupported generalities.

If we think of all the possible combinations of intelligence and creativity, we would find that there are four major combinations, which represent the extreme possibilities.

1. High intelligence and low creativity
2. High intelligence and high creativity
3. Low intelligence and high creativity
4. Low intelligence and low creativity

In between these four extremes there are many other shades of intelligence and creativity. With each combination there is a most effective approach.

While creative people tend to be more abstract, open-minded thinkers who are easily persuaded by the possibilities set forth in new ideas, concrete thinkers are more rigid, closed-minded, and difficult to persuade in any area.*

The most effective presentation for highly intelligent people will be one that is logically presented and that also represents open-minded, new-possibility thinking. Highly intelligent, non-creative people are more likely to be persuaded by strong logic and rigid, proven thinking rather than open-minded new thinking.

Less intelligent but highly creative people are influenced by emotional appeals and open-minded possibility thinking, which tends to make them vulnerable to unsupported arguments. Although less intelligent, noncreative people are also susceptible to emotional appeals, they do look for a greater degree of supporting factual documentation before they are persuaded.

The extreme approaches called for by these varying profiles would suggest that accurate audience profiling is essential for choosing the most effective presentation style. Consider the persuasive approach used to market beauty products, which plays intensively and exclusively to the emotional side of the audience. There is no real logic presented in any beauty marketing campaign that demonstrates that lipstick or any other cosmetic makes

*Ibid., p. 89.

a woman more beautiful or desirable. There is only the emotional appeal directed at a woman's interest in being attractive.

In contrast, the marketing approach, or persuasive technique, used to sell computer software is predominately a logical appeal to the intelligence and knowledge of the audience, who will choose one software product over another on the basis of what the product can do in terms of results and of how it might logically interact with other software already in place.

What a disaster it would be if salespeople were to try to market computer software on the basis of an emotional appeal, or women's beauty products on the basis of logic! A wrong audience diagnosis could result in a presentation style that would be fatal to the persuasion effort.

Managing Credibility Factors

An individual's credibility is initially gauged by the number and type of formal credentials, awards, and achievements he or she can claim. The more of these you have, and the closer they are tied to the argument you are presenting, the more initial credibility you may enjoy. However, following the initial exposure, your formal credentials tend to take a backseat in the eyes of the audience to what is perceived as your depth of operating knowledge on the topic. Eventually, the audience will assign you a level of credibility that it feels is appropriate. The higher your assigned credibility rating is, the greater the probability that your persuasive effort will be successful.*

This information would seem to argue for the recruitment of the most credible source to present your arguments on your behalf. For example, if you wanted to impress upon your sports-oriented son the importance of good academic grades as well as athletic achievement, you might arrange for the local football hero to deliver this message, because in the eyes of your child a football hero is a credible source.

The same is true in business and career situations. The targeted audience will be more receptive to hearing, believing, and remembering a message that is delivered by a source it views as

*Ibid., p. 108.

highly credible. Thus, the selection of a "champion" to present the message is an important part of persuasive strategy.

Not everyone can be viewed as the optimal credible source for every persuasive effort he needs to make—even when the ideas are his. So, when the credibility of the presenter, or some aspect of the core content, is in question, a work-around strategy is needed.

A work-around strategy is one that gets at the critical issues by "working around," or avoiding, what otherwise could become a barrier to the goal through using substitute strategies. "Negative selling" is an effective work-around strategy for presenters who are viewed as less than an expert in the field. This approach neutralizes any initial negative perceptions of a less than expert presenter.

The process of negative selling begins with the communicator presenting a strong persuasive case, and then, with equal zeal, pointing out to the audience the negative or questionable aspects of the proposal. By communicating the negative aspects in a way that highlights the relative strength of the attractive components of the proposal, the result is that audience members will challenge their own thinking and very likely persuade themselves to adopt the original proposal, given that the premises were strong to begin with.

Even in situations where the audience has been moved, or persuaded, to the desired opinion, negative selling assists in further solidifying the new opinion and preventing any backsliding or reversal in thinking. Therefore, the negative selling technique is recommended for use in every persuasive opportunity.

Positive or Negative Spin?

There are two approaches to presenting a persuasive argument. One is the positive argument in which logical facts build one upon another, and the focus of the argument is on the possibilities of the persuasive proposal. The second is a negative approach that focuses primarily, in an attacking type of mode, on the unattractive aspects of alternative competitive approaches in an effort to discredit competitors, and thus elevate the preferred argument to the primary position of choice.

Winning through a negative approach is like winning by default; it depends on disqualifying competing arguments rather than on emboldening the prescribed argument.

Psychologist Dr. Herbert Clark made a startling discovery as far back as 1976. Clark confirmed that it takes the average person about 48 percent longer to understand a negative statement than it does to understand a positive statement. This would suggest that more rapid persuasion occurs when concepts are presented in a constructive, positive manner, providing the concepts are logical and factual.

Every statement can be expressed either in a negative, demolishing manner or in a promising, positive manner. A deprecating delivery of the month-end report to your boss might sound something like this:

> Here it is. It's not as good as I thought it would be, but it's done.

These statements represent a negative, judgmental message, which would have been better left unsaid. Although specifically descriptive, the tough-sounding words make the message more difficult to hear. A more positive approach would be:

> Here is the report. I was hoping to make it look even better. Next month there will be more improvements.

The essence of the message is the same; the report has arrived, and there is room for improvement. However, the second approach is less judgmental, yet still descriptive, and uses a positive choice of words like "hoping" to persuade people to take action.

Daily communications, as well as critical persuasive efforts, are better received when they're built on positive, logical, credible factors of evidence rather than on the degradation of competing arguments that only sidetrack the focus of your presentation. Practice reconstructing negative thoughts into positive approaches and delivering unfavorable, or negative, messages in a constructive, suggestive, opportune manner.

Persuadability

A number of elements affect an argument's persuasiveness. Use the following list of persuadability factors to strategically create your plan of persuasion.

1. *Majority opinion.* People tend to act with the majority and are often reluctant to oppose it.* This suggests that information on the state of thinking of the majority of the audience is essential in preparing a persuasive effort. What opinions do the majority of people hold? How do these opinions relate to the argument you plan to present?

2. *Group identification.* People who are most attached to a group are probably the least influenced by communications that conflict with the group norms.** And people who are attached to a group tend to adopt group thinking. Therefore, knowledge of who is most attached, and who is least attached, to the group helps to target the message. Target messages of change to those least attached to the group because they are most likely to be persuaded and, in turn, being a part of the group, can persuade other group members.

3. *Personality traits.* Individual personality traits affect a person's susceptibility to persuasion. The authoritarian personality, which tends to have unquestioned respect for people in authority, such as parents, teachers, and bosses, is likely to be swayed by an appeal from an authority figure.[1] This suggests the importance of targeting authority figures in the initial stages of a persuasive appeal. Once their thinking is converted or solidified, the authority figure can make individual appeals to authoritarian personalities in the group and move their thinking to line up with the desired outcome.

Often, one-on-one private persuasive efforts occur prior to larger group presentations. The combination of authority figures and authoritarian figures, successfully converted to your way of thinking, represents a larger mass of people, approaching a majority.

---

* Ibid., p. 44.
** Ibid., p. 57.
[†] Ibid., p. 99.

4. *Patience and persuasion.* Few persuasive efforts conclude rapidly. Attempts to rush a persuasive process can become distractions to the process and the audience and will sometimes result in a derailed or failed effort. Have patience with each step of a persuasive strategy. Take the time needed to build the bridges, putting each piece of the persuasive puzzle into place.

5. *Strategic planning for persuasion.* A large audience is not likely to be persuaded as a group all at one time. Interrelationships of various audience members, the personality profiles of the audience, and the current state of mind of audience leaders and authority figures must all be addressed in proper sequence. Much like the domino effect and the toppling over of the first dominoes, the persuasion of key figures can set off a chain reaction of changed thinking that will affect all those they are associated with. Conversely, inaccurate sequencing could result in an effort that is blocked by conflicting opinions in key people who have not been given the appropriate persuasive information and attention.

To prepare your persuasive strategy, analyze the key decision makers, thought leaders, and informal audience leaders. Gear your persuasive strategy to them initially. Then, in conjunction with this larger, persuaded body of influencers, strategize appropriate behaviors and communications to change the thinking and behavior of the balance of the audience.

6. *Bridge building and barrier breakdown.* Some barriers are material, requiring a physical action to remove or change them, for example, the barrier between management and staff as represented by privileged parking spaces for managers. To break this barrier requires only the elimination of a policy and/or the physical removal of the privileged parking sign. Other barriers are grounded in differences in perception. To persuade is to change perceptions. People are more readily persuaded by a communicator they perceive to be similar to themselves.*

This suggests that a key element of all persuasive strategies is to find, or develop, as many common links as possible between yourself and the audience in the following areas:

- Opinions
- Goals

*Ibid., p. 128.

- Experiences
- Challenges
- Personal profile elements
- Types of work you do
- Where you live
- Personal hobbies and interests

7. *Audience participation.* Participation and involvement serve the dual purposes of keeping the communicator informed of the audience's present state of mind, even as it is evolving, while at the same time providing the audience with an opportunity to shape one another's perspectives as well as the final outcome. All this is orchestrated and directed by the communicator through the use of audience participation.

Audience participation can take the form of:

- Voting by voice or physical gesture. Ways of soliciting audience feedback include stating, "By way of a hand up, how many people think..." or, "By raising your hand, let's see how many think..."
- Generating lists of answers to a question posed by the presenter
- Physically doing some activity in conjunction with the audience leader
- Processing small group discussions. This is a breakout of the audience into small workable groups of six to ten people each, who are then given some work activity to complete as a group
- Interactive questions and answers
- Role playing by audience members
- Creating action plans in teams

8. *Word delivery.* Strategic use of a few small words such as *we, you,* and *I* make the difference between a message being favorably received and a message that is never received.

We is the most important word in a persuasive effort. Engaging, yet ambiguous, the word *we* connotes the inclusion of everyone, the presenter and the audience as a part of a unified group. It is simultaneously a barrier breaker and a bridge builder. Abraham Lincoln used *we* in his famous Gettysburg Address: "We are met on a great battlefield…" Knute Rockne used *we* to invite teamwork, not stardom. You can use *we* to bring yourself closer to the audience.

We also implies numbers of people, and numbers of people imply strength and power. Therefore, the use of *we* creates a more powerful image. Use *we* and *our* when referring to yourself in any context. For example, when referencing your work you might say, "in our work…we do it this way…" rather than saying "in my work…." Or, "we feel that this is the best alternative because…" rather than "I feel…." Avoid the lonely word *I*, which, standing alone, is vulnerable to attack.

You is an important word in persuasive conversation because it speaks directly to a person. People hearing the message directed at them receive a more personalized message, even when they are part of a crowd, because *you* is personal and individual.

9. *Attention grabbers*. There are about a dozen words that when used by a credible source will gain immediate audience attention. Most of these words are recognizable from their frequent use in consumer product advertising campaigns. They are frequently used because they are effective. A selective combination of a number of these powerful words in your communication will gain the attention of the audience. Be careful not to use the words falsely or too often, which would dilute their effect.

Attention-Gaining Headline Words

guarantee	money	results
new	save	proven
easy	uncover	love
health	safety	you

10. *Change opportunity*. For those targeted audience members who are formulating their first opinion, a change opportunity is not needed because they are not changing anything. However, if you are trying to create a change of opinion in audience members, a gracious change opportunity is necessary, one in which they can change their minds or opinions easily without losing face.

The First Is Not the Last Position

Opinions do not move dramatically from one position to another without undergoing several intermediate evaluative processes, frequently nudged by such factors as group norms, appeals to authority, and fear. Persuasion is an evolutionary process. The opinions of people are growing and changing.

Because the sequence of influencing events is not always controllable or anticipated, you must realize that the first position or point of view that an audience holds is not necessarily its final position. An indefinite number of opinions will evolve in the interim. The challenge and goal is to advantageously manage the landslide of influencing factors in order to ensure that the desired position is the last position—and to shield that desired position from influencers that could change it further. To maintain the desired opinion state, use three techniques:

1. Repeat persuasive appeals.
2. Seek specific audience participation.
3. Consistently reinforce the correctness of the new opinion through credible, positive feedback.

Duration of the Effects of Persuasion Techniques

Research indicates that the effects of persuasive communication tend to wear off.* The speed with which they wear off is dependent on a number of factors, including:

- The length of time following the initial communication
- The immediate effectiveness of the message
- The extent to which the audience believes the statements to be true

The effects of persuasion tend to wear off in direct proportion to the amount of time that has elapsed. The more time that goes by, the greater the decay of the opinion change is. However, the greater the effectiveness of the original message, the greater the residual effects will be. And to the extent that the audience believes the statements to be true, the greater the possibility is that your message will be recalled rather than forgotten.**

---

* Ibid., p. 70.
** Ibid., pp. 72–73.

Profile of the Effective Communicator

Achieving the goal of successful persuasion requires recruitment of the most effective communicator, one who is specifically matched to the audience profile and argument topic. In choosing the most effective communicator, consider the following checklist.

- ❏ *Credibility.* It's easier to persuade when you are credible and trusted than it is when you are unknown and therefore not trusted. Is the selected communicator highly credible to the target audience?
- ❏ *Intelligence.* Highly intelligent audiences relate more quickly to highly intelligent presenters. Is the presentation style reflective of a logical, intelligent presenter?
- ❏ *Passion versus emotionalism.* Passion for the persuasive argument is an asset. Emotion is a liability. Will the presenter control the passion and emotion exhibited and use the passion wisely?
- ❏ *Information.* In order to connect with the audience, the presenter must know the audience profile. What are the burning issues for this group? Which are sensitive issues? What are its perspectives, goals, and challenges? Who are its leaders? And how does the organizational culture operate?
- ❏ *Facts.* Is the presenter's material well documented and factual?
- ❏ *Control.* Calmness is inviting. Emotionalism is distracting.
- ❏ *Extroversion.* Is the presenter prepared to speak up spontaneously when there is a need to control unexpected audience responses?
- ❏ *Connection.* Is the presenter someone that audience thought leaders and authority figures can easily connect with?
- ❏ *Understanding.* Is the presenter capable of showing an understanding of the audience and of the persuasive process that would be most effective with this particular audience?
- ❏ *Strategic thinking.* Does the presenter thoroughly understand the strategy of persuasion for this particular audience, and is he capable of quickly adapting his persuasive efforts to audience reactions in order to maximize results?

Part Four

Prescriptive Behaviors to Make Yourself Memorable

"The art of living rightly is like all arts; it must be learned and practiced with incessant care."

—Goethe

Everyone has the potential to become memorable. The secret of the success lies in understanding the factors and applying the strategies already discussed. Application of an appropriate strategy, boosted with M factors, will guarantee a memorable event. But what if you don't have time to read the principles and practices described in earlier chapters? What if you need immediate, action-oriented behaviors? Then Part Four is for you.

The following chapters point to explicit behaviors and action-oriented ideas for making yourself memorable to your targeted audiences of customers, bosses, family, and friends. Use these ideas as a starting point to change your behavior and develop a more positive and memorable image. Take each concept and develop it further along the lines that are geared specifically to your targeted audience. Consider the purpose behind each idea, then translate that purpose into additional action items that are appropriate for your audience. Remember that some one-time events have the potential to become memorable, but more often it is the whole package of behaviors that will create the lasting desirable impact.

8

Make Yourself
Memorable to Customers

*"It is the customer, and the customer alone, who casts the
vote that determines how big any company should be..."*

—Crawford H. Grenwalt

The success or failure of most businesses is in large part attributable to the successful or failed function of customer management. Broader in scope than customer satisfaction, the concept of customer management includes the ideas of recruitment, retention, and nurturing of the customer base. Those organizations that manage customer relationships will be successful. Those that do not, will not.

What do customers want? That is the essential question in business. Customers are universally simple-minded in many respects. They all want some of the same things. When you give them what they want, they will come. When they get what they want, they are happy. The more you give them of what they want, the happier they will be. The happier they are, the more friends they tell. The more friends they tell, the busier your business will be. The busier your business is, the more successful you become, and the more resources you will have to do the things that customers want.

There are five universal customer expectations, as shown in Figure 8-1. These are the things that all customers desire, the things that will make all customers feel satisfied.

Customers expect to find these five characteristics in each business encounter. When any one of the five is less than

Figure 8-1   Universal customer expectations.

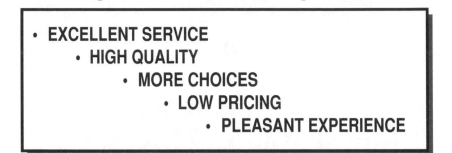

- **EXCELLENT SERVICE**
  - **HIGH QUALITY**
    - **MORE CHOICES**
      - **LOW PRICING**
        - **PLEASANT EXPERIENCE**

acceptable from the customer perspective, they will rank the overall experience as unsatisfactory. When all five characteristics are simultaneously in place, a peak memorable customer experience occurs. *The goal of a memorable organization is to consistently create peak customer experiences for each customer in every encounter.*

The Master Strategy

If a peak customer experience is the universal goal, then the challenge is to determine which strategies, behaviors, and actions are required to create that experience.

There is but one strategy for creating peak customer experiences and that is to *exceed customer expectations.*

Although this formula for exceeding customer expectations seems simple and straightforward enough, it becomes more complex when we realize that these expectations are further defined by each individual customer. For example, customer A's service expectations might be a fast, friendly, and knowledgeable service staff, whereas customer B has a much higher and more explicit level of expectation associated with the concept of customer service, and customer C has still a different expectation of service levels. There are an infinite number of levels and definitions of what "exceeding customer expectations" could mean. How can an organization or individual staff member consistently exceed all customer expectations when the number and types of expectations are so varied?

In order to exceed service expectations for all customers, the highest and most exalted level of service must consistently be provided to all customers. In order to meet this extreme level of service, the following strategies are proposed. Notice that each strategy is related to one or more of the M factors previously discussed in Chapter 5.

There are four strategic service initiatives that are universally recommended to transform present service levels into extraordinary service levels. Use the following principles to direct your thinking and to turn these ideas into concrete initiatives for your organization.

1. Consistently employ the tactics of "firsts" and "bests."
   - *The first to offer a service or product.* Kinko's Copy Centers were the first to offer twenty-four-hour, full-service office equipment and support centers, thus adopting the strategy of being the first to provide this type and level of service.
   - *Faster service.* Domino Pizza's thirty-minute delivery standard was faster service than other competitors provided.
   - *The best service.* Patients of Holy Cross Hospital in Chicago rate their health care experience there as being the *best*. This is evident by the consistently superior customer satisfaction ratings from the patients at Holy Cross.
   - *More prompt service.* When customers walk in the supplier's door, is there someone there to serve them immediately?
   - *More thorough service.* Northwest Oilers auto center does more than change the oil in your car. Its mechanics routinely check and repair all auto fluids and air pressure needs as part of the oil change process. They give your vehicle a thorough fluid checkup, not just a change of oil.
   - *More convenient service.* Walmart and Meirs superstores are designed with the idea of one-stop shopping in mind. Groceries, soft goods, electronics, entertainment—anything you might need for daily living—is under one roof for convenience.
   - *More personalized service.* In Nordstrom Stores, a consumer retailing organization, it is not uncommon to find

sales associates who have developed personal relationships with their customers. They call them by name,
know their preferences in colors, styles, and manufacturers, and maintain some level of ongoing communication with them regarding new product arrivals or
special events that the customer might be interested in.
The level of service that Nordstrom's provides is more
than the five-minute, onetime transaction commonly
experienced at other comparable retailers.

- *More knowledgeable and trained service people.*

2. *Add elements of "distinction."* To be distinctive is to be different from the rest. What service, or elements of service, can
you provide that are distinctively different from what others are
doing? For example, a grocer who delivers food to your home or
a car repair service that washes your car before returning it to
you are examples of distinctive elements of service, elements
that few, if any other, competitors provide.

Beware of copycat efforts. As quickly as you adopt new, distinctive elements, competitors will copy them. The effort to
remain distinctive is an eternal process.

3. *Make no assumptions.* Assumptions are dangerous. Just
when the answer seems obvious, reality proves that the correct
answer is anything but the obvious one. To find out what is in
the hearts and minds of your customers, you must ask them.
Surveys, questionnaires, focus groups, and being among the
customers, that is, management by walking around, are effective
models for soliciting feedback.

4. *Listen for opportunities.* Customers are generally willing to
tell us what is wrong with our service and how we can improve it.
Unfortunately, we are not always interested in listening. Listen
carefully to everything customers say. What they say they like
about your service is as important as what they say they don't
like. Do more of what they like, and stop doing what they don't
like. Use listening skills to identify new distinctive, desirable elements of customer service. The customer will tell you what to do.

Suggestions for Exceeding Service Expectations

The most effective suggestions for exceeding a specific customer's service expectations will come directly from that cus-

tomer. However, there are a number of universal customer service expectations. The following list is based on the recommendations of routine shoppers and can serve as your tip sheet on ways to exceed customer service expectations.

1. *Provide immediate product location information.* Why is it generally so difficult to find a particular product in either small or large stores? Immediate product location is a matter of convenience and efficiency for the supplier and the customer.

2. *Provide no-wait checkout service.* Customers shouldn't have to wait to give away their money. But isn't that what happens when people have to stand in a checkout line?

3. Provide easy access, including:

- Doors that open automatically.
- Convenient parking and entry.
- One-stop shopping and corresponding support services.
- Product selection that is retrieved.
- The possibility of ordering at any time and from any location—home, office, car, or while traveling. Ours is a fast-paced society in which time is at a premium. When the customer is limited to a specific time and/or location to place an order, chances are that not all possible customers can conform to those time frames. Thus, sales and customers are lost to competitors who match or exceed what you offer, and in a more convenient way.

4. *Avoid out-of-stock situations.*

5. *Offer repair work at the purchase site, along with loaners during repair times.* When the VCR purchase is made at one location, repair work and loaners should also be available at that same location. Not only is this a customer convenience, but it creates the sense of an ongoing relationship with the supplier. The stronger the relationship becomes, the greater the customer's patience will be should future disappointments or mistakes occur.

6. *Provide immediate and accurate answers to product questions.* The computer software industry is a good example of superior service and information processing. Software companies quickly provide accurate answers to technical questions by centralizing all product questions with a team of highly trained, well equipped, competent staff members.

7. *Make customized products available upon request.*

8. *Have a continuing contact with the customer.* Advise customers when new product designs or accessories, which they may be interested in, become available. Every three months, as the seasons change, the woman's shoe salon at Nordstrom's Department Store contacts customers to report on the various styles arriving for the new season. It offers to ship shoes to your home for approval with no necessity on your part to make a commitment. If you like them and want to keep them, they are charged to your account, but if you choose to return them, there is no charge or hassle. The continuing contact provides a convenience to the customer and builds sales for the organization.

9. *Offer "try before you buy" opportunities.* These are opportunities for customers to try, or test-drive, products or services before making a buying commitment. The "try before you buy" experience soothes purchasing anxiety, making the total experience more pleasant and allowing the customer to make a more informed, and therefore more confident, buying decision.

10. *Provide on-site service for installation, assembly, and product performance demonstration.*

Create your list of behaviors and activities that are designed to exceed customer service expectations. To do this, first define what your customers' service expectations are. Then, ask customers for specific examples of what they would consider to be extraordinary customer service. Remember, make no assumptions. What the customer asks for is what the customer values. Take these ideas and develop them further to create a truly exceptional service experience.

Service Killers

The best executed service program can quickly dissolve in the wake of a few, and sometimes only one, of the following service killer situations. Even when everything else is being done correctly, one service killer can cause the loss of a sale, a customer, or an image. Common service killers are:

1. *Products being out of stock.* A full and complete inventory eliminates customer defection to competitors who can provide immediate product delivery.

2. *Product ignorance.* Employees need to be knowledgeable about all aspects of products that are available to the customer. Product information allows the customer to make an intelligent and informed choice, which in turn reflects on how the customer feels about the organization. Product ignorance is like a statement from the supplier that says, "Here it is, figure it out for yourself."

3. *Absence of the personal, human touch.* Rapid automation calls for caution. Do not lose sight of the personal element necessary in every customer transaction. Processes and systems can be automated, but somewhere in the chain of transactions a personal intervention must be available. At the point that automation completely replaces the human element, the opportunity to be distinctive has been diminished, and all customers will be reduced to one common denominator and treated the same way—with no distinction.

4. *Waiting lines.* Time is the customer's most precious and limited commodity; therefore people don't like to wait for anything. A great many customer defections occur because people do not have the time or patience to wait. They often would rather do without, or seek another provider, than wait.

5. *A do-it-yourself mentality.* Although do-it-yourself centers are popular, it is the supplies that can be purchased there that determine their success. Organizations that leave things for the customer to do that the organization could just as well do for them are flirting with market share defeat. People want things to be done for them. Serve the customer.

6. *No delivery options.* Not everything the customer wants or needs will fit into the trunk of a car. Organizations that offer to sell a product but do not provide delivery are missing a market opportunity. Be prepared to deliver anything you are prepared to sell.

7. *No on-site assistance.* The number of business transactions will be reduced when there is no one to assist customers to find things or show them how they work.

Strategies for Exceeding Quality Expectations

Customer quality expectations are universally the same; to consistently receive a flawless product or service. Exceeding customer quality expectations is a workable strategy for making yourself memorable so long as the following two initiatives are simultaneously undertaken:

1. You make flawless quality your goal.
2. You find some distinctive element associated with the quality goal.

Flawlessness alone is not enough to set you apart from the competitive crowd. Some element of distinctiveness is needed. This is the sizzle on the steak. Rolls Royce automobile manufacturers seek flawless quality in their products, and support this initiative with lifetime warranties—something that no other automobile company even closely approximates. The lifetime warranty exemplifies initiatives of both flawless quality and distinctiveness.

The following prescriptions will help you to create your action plan to exceed quality expectations.

1. *Deal with the best.* Be selective in your choice of supportive vendors. Low-quality inputs result in low-quality outcomes. High-quality inputs result in high-quality outcomes. Use only high-quality products and services that you can count on. Cost cutting on quality inputs results in profit cutting for product outputs.

2. *Implement a "no questions asked" policy.* If flawless quality has not been achieved, then prepare to do the next best thing— make the quality correction encounter as pleasant and convenient for the customer as possible. All quality issues should be quickly remedied to the customer's satisfaction, "no questions asked."

3. *Install the most extensive warranty/guarantee program.* Longer and more extensive warranties imply better quality and give customers a greater sense of customer confidence. Go for lifetime warranties or satisfaction guaranteed programs that are hassle-free for the customer and easy for staff members to administer.

4. *Boast of your successes.* Publicize quality awards and recognition received. People want to be associated with winners. At the time St. Mary's Medical Center was named as one of the "100 Best Hospitals," 1994, the staff created enormous signs to hang on the exterior and interior of the facility to publicize the

award and to communicate to current and potential hospital patients the superior quality of the hospital.

All awards, letters of recognition or appreciation, and winning trophies that you receive should be prominently displayed.

Recovering From a Quality Disappointment

There is only one way to exceed customer quality expectations, and that is to outlive the customer. Regardless of utilization, the customer expects the product or service to last longer than it has or will.

Because there are few products that exceed customers' increasingly more demanding quality expectations, it is necessary to be prepared to handle quality issues in a memorable and pleasant way.

The following recommendations are designed to create a smooth and pleasant recovery from a customer's quality problem. Use the recommendations as a starting point in your thinking to create a smooth transition from customer disappointment to exceeding customer expectations. Remember, the goal is to transform the damaging quality event into a memorable and positive experience for the customer.

1. *Offer a sincere apology for the inconvenience.* Augment the verbal apology with an "apology pack." We first learned of this idea from Northwest Airlines whose flight attendants are equipped with apology packs to help soothe unexpected customer irritations. The apology pack can include any number of items, for example, a discount on the next service or visit, or a complimentary service or visit, whichever is more appealing. Also consider some fun item to distract the customer from obsessing on the problem situation. The idea is to provide something of value more than a verbal apology.

2. *Deliver a replacement product to the customer.* The customer is already irritated with the defective product or service. Do not require him to go through further inconveniences in order to have the situation corrected. The inconvenience caused by poor quality should be absorbed by the provider. Deliver a complimentary replacement, or temporary replacement product or service, to the customer's home, office, or selected location.

3. *Follow up.* Follow up personally with the customer to ensure that the replacement or temporary product meets or exceeds the customer's performance expectations. Any further disappointments require instant attention. At this stage, any further defects will reinforce the initial negative experience rather than correct it.

Strategies for Exceeding Choice Expectations

Customers expect to be presented with an adequate number of choices or options in their buying experience. The greater the number of customer choices you offer, the more likely you are to exceed customer choice expectations, making the experience a memorable one. When the number or type of choices is less than expected, people feel disappointed, and are likely to defect to competitors where other choices are perceived to better meet their expectations, or at least fill the void created in their initial experience with you.

The idea of exceeding customer choice expectations is an approach currently used by specialty marketers to gain a distinctive market niche advantage. Best Buy electronic superstores are an example of exploiting multiple choices at the consumer retail level. The Best Buy concept is to offer customers the most extensive choice of consumer electronic options available under one roof. When properly executed, this strategy creates an overwhelmingly positive effect. However, if the strategy is executed in a less than excellent way, the memorable impact will be overwhelmingly negative. Distinctive applications of this marketing niche strategy are becoming more prevalent as we see automobile malls, retail sports centers, and specialty luggage stores among the examples of organizations sporting a full range of customer choices in a historically departmentalized area.

In preparing your personal action plan to exceed customer choice expectations, consider including the following ideas:

1. *A full range of options.* A large number of choices also means a full range of choices. "Full range" refers to both ends of the choice spectrum and everything in between. The most expensive and the least expensive. The most sophisticated and

the least sophisticated. Traditional versus modern versions. A strategic error would be to limit choices toward one end of the spectrum or to eliminate a section of product choices. Expand the choices to the maximum.

2. *"Try before you buy opportunities."* Such opportunities are important in the comparative decision-making process, which is what choices are all about. The "try before you buy" tactic has always been in place in the automobile market, where customers expect to test-drive the product, but has been less aggressively applied in other areas of purchasing. Recently put in place at Blockbuster Music stores, "try before you buy" equipment allows customers to listen to any musical product in advance of the purchase and without a commitment to buy or any hassle. There is a surefire way to ensure customer satisfaction and to reduce the number of returned products owing to customer disappointment. Expand the "try before you buy" opportunities into every product and service line. Do not be deferred by conventional practices.

3. *Easy-to-maneuver situations.* Create friendly environments in which it is easy for people to roam the aisles and review the choices. Crowded, cluttered, and clumsily designed environments are barrier builders for customers, and often shorten the buying trip, translating into lost sales and a damaged image.

4. *Adding accessories.* Accessories expand the sense of having many choices beyond the basic product options. Numerous combinations of accessories with products create a greater number of product choices. Maximize the number of choices by mixing and matching accessories and products.

Choice Killers

Maximum customer choice often means maximum inventory levels, and the financial implications thereof, which in turn cause managers to falsely rationalize the inventory on hand. The challenge of exceeding customer choice expectations is to find an appropriate balance between customer choice options and financial viability. Hence, the introduction of catalog buying, which limits the need for on-hand inventory if just-in-time inventory is available, and the explosive growth in specialty suppliers.

If the objective is to supply the fullest range of customer choices, the obvious choice killer behaviors would be:

1. Representation of a limited price range for products.
2. Representation of a limited number of manufacturers or suppliers.
3. Representation of a limited number of styles of product.
4. Representation of a limited number of colors or sizes of product.

Strategies for Exceeding Pricing Expectations

People have gone cost-crazy. The concept of cost management permeates personal and professional objectives, dominating both national and local news stories. Consequently, there is a heightened sense of price/value relationships.

People have a preconceived idea of the price and value of an item, of the price/value relationship. The preconceived cost and the real cost are sometimes the same. But sometimes they are dramatically different.

When the real cost of an item is less than the preconceived cost, the customer's pricing expectation is exceeded, and a favorably memorable event is likely to occur.

When real costs are substantially greater than preconceived costs, sticker shock sets in, and the customer becomes disenchanted with the purchasing situation, and sometimes disenchanted with your organization by association. The disenchantment will likely cause her to leave in search of alternative suppliers or solutions. This sale is lost, and possibly future sales to this customer may be lost for life.

Because of the inherent constraints of pricing, that is, the need to make a profit, and the key role of pricing in the customer's decision-making process, the strategy of exceeding pricing expectations must be fluid, adaptable to meet individual customer expectations.

The most fluid and individually customer-oriented pricing is one that is philosophical in nature, and individual in application: the "guaranteed lowest price" tactic.

This pricing tactic, sometimes called the "we won't be undersold" approach, seeks to exceed every customer's price expectation. It operates just as it sounds. When the customer can prove that within a reasonable geographical distance, the identical product is being sold elsewhere for less, then our price will be reduced x percent, or dollars, lower than the competitor's price—a guaranteed lowest price.

Guaranteed lowest pricing benefits the supplier because customers are assured that their pricing expectations will be consistently met, and the organization can do this without the additional overhead costs of promotion, or loss of income from customers who are willing to pay the higher price.

Price Killers

There is one thing that is certain to destroy a customer relationship if it occurs with any degree of regularity. That destructive behavior is called overpricing—pricing identical products or services significantly higher than competitors do without providing some additional value to justify the greater cost.

Not every organization engages in overpricing, but all organizations have the potential to do so. At the point overpricing is discovered by the customer, the customer/supplier relationship ends. It is as if a betrayal of the customer has occurred, a betrayal of the implied price/value "contract" the customer had trusted in.

The fine jewelry department of a famous department store has earned this disheartening reputation. For several years this store was on the shopping list of places to check as I helped friends and family members select precious anniversary gifts. The first comparative shopping experience exposed its pricing to be nearly double that of its competitor. Imagine which organization got that sale. The following year, I consulted this organization again. This time the situation was even more extreme, its "on sale" pricing being significantly higher than that of its competitors' normal pricing.

Thinking that there might be some error or unawareness on the part of the store manager, I brought this to her attention, showing her the exact product I had purchased at a competing store, along with the receipt. Now, you might think that the manager would at least have attempted to fake some surprise or offer some excuse. But there was nothing. No response at all!

This repetitive overpricing and the nonresponsive management cost this famous retailer these two sales, as well as *all* future sales of what once was a lifetime customer. No longer is there a customer/supplier trust relationship with this store.

Unless your organization offers a product or service that is so unique that it is not offered by any other organization at any time, customer retention and recruitment calls for competitive pricing at a minimum, and preferably extraordinary pricing to exceed customer expectations.

Creating a Memorable "Personal Experience"

The copycat nature of customer service, quality, choices, and pricing initiatives can leave competitive organizations that are doing all the right things in an undistinguishable position. When each new strategy or initiative put into place is quickly copied by a competitor, what is left to distinguish your organization from others? The answer to this question is what separates excellent organizations from good organizations. The answer is the delivery of a "personal experience."

A "personal experience" is what a customer undergoes from the first encounter with an organization to the final encounter. It can be a memorable experience, one exceeding expectations, or, it can be a "dis" experience—disheartening, disappointing, and despairing. Your objective is to avoid the "dis" experiences and to create an entirely pleasant personal experience for your customers from start to finish.

Recipe for a Memorable "Personal Experience"

Memorable experiences grow out of an accumulation of many small things going as expected or better than expected. To create memorable experiences for your customers, consider the following prescriptions:

1. *Personalize everything.*
   - Call customers by name.
   - Praise or compliment customers honestly and frequently.

- Know personal preference details. In the hotel business, the Marriott Hotels chain maintains a customer profile of its Club Marquis members—customers who use Marriott facilities fairly frequently. Room preferences and special requests are known and prepared for in advance of each guest's arrival. They know your personal preferences right down to the type of soft drinks you consumed on your last visit.
- Stock a good brand of complimentary coffee.
- Stock an unusual complimentary snack item—pickles, peanuts in the shell, jelly beans, lemon drops, you name it.
- Celebrate a personal event, like a birthday or wedding anniversary, with the customer.
- Energize the environment.
  —Pump oxygen into the air to keep it fresh.
  —Keep the temperature cool but comfortable.
  —Generate activity in the environment—many people, music, hustle and bustle.
- Know the history of customers' past encounters with your organization. What types of purchases and returns have they made? What services have been rendered?
- Provide personal contact information. Give each customer a card with your name and business telephone number on it as well as the name and telephone number of the manager. Executives are not the only people who need business cards.
- Make personal Thanksgiving Day calls on your customers to thank them for their past business.
- Use caller ID services to answer the phone so you can address the customer by name.
- Send holiday greeting cards. Enclose your photo together with a handwritten personal message. Avoid preprinted messages. Personal messages take more time to create, but are much more meaningful.
- Provide complimentary valet or personal parking.
- Provide an entertainment section to occupy the children while their parents are transacting business.
- Provide complimentary delivery services.

- Provide complimentary wheelchairs for shopping convenience.
- Provide complimentary baby strollers.
- Provide a customer lounge for frequent buyers.

2. *Make it fun.* Creating an environment that has some element of fun associated with it is one way for people to make themselves or their business memorable. McDonald's hamburger outlets turned leisure eating into a recreational event with the inauguration of playgrounds, happy meals, toys, and paper hats. Southwest Airlines uses comedic telephone marketing messages to entertain as well as inform customers who are "on hold." The Saturn automobile manufacturing plant holds an annual picnic for all Saturn customers. Tens of thousands of people attend. What can you do to add fun to the business experience? Consider these approaches:

- Add humor to your messages.
- Host widely attended social events—fairs, picnics, celebrations, sporting and other community-oriented activities.
- Be spontaneous.

3. *Solve a problem.* Do whatever is needed to solve customers' problems, relieving their anxieties and allowing a pleasant relationship to continue. Train staff to use such ingratiating phrases as:

- "I'd like to solve this for you now."
- "No problem."
- "Of course."
- "If it would please you."
- "It would make us happy to solve this problem for you."

4. *Entertain.* Customers like to be entertained. Audio, video, personal, and self-directed entertainment opportunities are effective. No matter what your business environment or industry, these entertainment ideas work.

- A pianist playing both golden oldies and contemporary favorites
- Multiple video messages and screens

- Seasonal musical messages
- Product demonstrators
- Relaxation and rest centers
- Action-oriented advertising—messages that move, glitter, and swing
- Interactive product or service education and information
- Costumes and thematic uniforms for workers, where appropriate
- Virtual reality experiences
- Remote shopping access
- Unique lighting and wall designs
- Artistic decor, including paintings and sculpture
- Interesting architectural elements
- Bright colors
- On-site challenges and competitions
- A chorus singing
- Soloists, quartets, and other musical combinations
- Theme days
- Free samples of products and services
- Air made fragrant by citrus, floral, or other fresh scents
- Play areas with equipment and supplies to occupy children
- A view of "behind the scenes" preparation, for example, glass wall partitions through which customers can observe:
  —Chefs cooking in a restaurant
  —Jewelers examining precious stones in a jewelry store
  —Butchers cutting meat in a supermarket
  —Auto mechanics at work in a car dealership
  —Children at play in a day care center
  —Athletes competing in a sports center
  —Lab technicians conducting experiments in a laboratory

Observation is both entertaining and informative; it provides a sense of the quality of the product or service being offered. What entertainment opportunities can you provide?

5. *Be thoughtful.*
   - Display good manners. Politeness saves energy.
   - Don't rush or seem hurried. Take the time the customer needs.
   - Balance air circulation. Avoid hot or cold blasts.
   - Have wide, unencumbered walking aisles.
   - Install mirrors for clear reflection.
   - Offer gathering areas where people can rest or engage in conversation.
   - Place an easy chair by each dressing room or area where time is needed for customers to come to a decision.
   - Provide drinking water facilities with cups.
   - Ensure access to the handicapped.
   - Offer customer assistance with heavy or awkward purchases.
   - Provide service in any location—office, home, or traveling bus, wherever the customer wants to have it.
   - Inquire as to any personal needs, then fill them.

6. *Create desirability.*
   - Offer a limited edition. Exclusivity creates desire.
   - Promote uniqueness, one-of-a-kind characteristics.
   - Communicate in the positive. Ban the word *no* from your vocabulary. If a nonaffirmative response is called for, say it in a positive way.
   - Limit availability, for instance, by advertising merchandise as "Available only in Chicago" or "Available only at this location."
   - Don't push the product—present it. If it is good, and the right thing for the customer, it will be desirable.
   - Find a need and fill it.

Desirability is contagious. In this me-too world, some desirability generates greater desirability. It is a self-perpetuating process that only needs a start.

Personal Experience Killers

The category of customer expectations that is most difficult to manage is that of an individual "personal experience." If all else goes well, but some aspect of the personal experience is unpleasant, the value of the entire encounter is diminished.

First-time personal experience killers are not always relationship killers. In some cases, customers will tolerate a poor personal experience, or even a number of them, for a period of time before they defect. There is, however, a limit to anyone's tolerance for unpleasantness.

Certain things are surefire personal experience killers, among which can be listed:

- Rude people (including rude customers as well as rude employees)
- Inconsiderate people
- Gossipy people
- Boredom (as in warehouse shopping)
- Customer-unfriendly facilities (such as inadequate parking facilities or difficult-to-access entrances)
- High expectations that are unfulfilled
- Inconsistent performance levels (as between different employees and different departments within one store)

Fickle Customers

Customer loyalty is a passing concept. Customers are loyal only to the extent that they are satisfied with their last transaction. To retain a constant customer base, or develop a larger one, requires the ability to consistently provide peak customer experiences.

Fickleness in the customer population can also work to your advantage if you have followed the prescriptions thus far. Because unsatisfied customers will move from one supplier to the next until they find satisfaction, dissatisfaction with competitors could mean a new customer opportunity for you.

New customer opportunities arise when:

1. *People talk favorably about their experience with you.* Good news travels fast. In our me-too environment, everybody wants to be or have the best, therefore they will seek you out when they hear of the extraordinary experience you offer.
2. *Competitors' customers become dissatisfied with their performance and seek out alternative sources.* In this situation, you are likely be given a trial opportunity.

3. *You offer products or services that cannot be acquired elsewhere.*
4. *The personal experience exceeds customer expectations.*
5. *New customer needs are identified and filled.*

Creating peak experiences is an ongoing, dynamically evolving process. There is no time at which you can afford to become comfortable with the status quo, even when the current performance level is considered to be the best. You can be sure that someone is always working harder and longer in the interest of overcoming your leadership position. To get ahead, and then stay ahead, means continual improvements and constant change.

9

Make Yourself Memorable to Your Boss

"There are few, if any, jobs in which ability alone is sufficient. Needed, also, are loyalty, sincerity, enthusiasm and team play."

—*William B. Given, Jr.*

Getting ahead means getting noticed and becoming indispensable in this throwaway world. Strategies for making yourself indispensable depend on the type of boss or other decision-making group involved.

Types of Bosses

Bosses come in as many varieties as there are ice cream flavors. However, six basic types of bosses seem to predominate (see Figure 9-1).

Your boss may exactly fit into one of the categories described, or he or she may be a combination of more than one type. Understanding the needs of each type, then strategizing on how to meet and exceed their expectations in a distinguishable manner is one way to make yourself memorable and indispensable. Let's look at each category of boss with an open view as to what is intended by these generalizations.

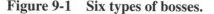

Figure 9-1   Six types of bosses.

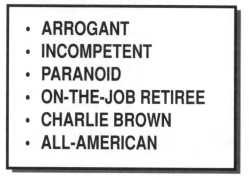

- **ARROGANT**
- **INCOMPETENT**
- **PARANOID**
- **ON-THE-JOB RETIREE**
- **CHARLIE BROWN**
- **ALL-AMERICAN**

The Arrogant Boss

The arrogant boss is a person who has pretensions to, or makes unwarranted claims to, superior importance or rights. She treats others in a subordinate manner, and is often self-absorbed with her self-appointed importance, making her difficult to talk to and work with. Notice the number of references to "self" in the description of the arrogant boss.

Usually competent in their work, but out of touch with their true level of importance, arrogant bosses focus only on what they think will make them look good to their boss and others above them in the hierarchy. They are not particularly receptive to ideas for improvement unless they themselves are the source of the new idea. Often they have few close relationships with colleagues because their arrogant nature causes others to keep a distance from them.

The Incompetent Boss

This type of boss cannot adequately do the work he is responsible for. Attempts at work either result in less than satisfactory outcomes or consume more time than normally would be needed.

Generally, this person is blind to his incompetence and highly sensitive to any approach that might suggest such inadequacies. He does not hold himself accountable for problems in work, being quick to blame someone or something else for any difficulties or flaws that are encountered. The work results of the incompetent boss define his level of competency. A laboratory supervisor who does not follow prescribed testing procedures because of a lack of knowledge or lack of ability, thereby rendering the test results questionable at best, is an example of an incompetent boss.

Incompetent people seem to have an excuse for each act of incompetence, a defensive approach that grows out of the endless excuses they have become accustomed to giving. Aggressive support staff and highly competent people are often viewed as threatening by incompetent people. Perhaps it is the threat of having their incompetency exposed that causes the dislike.

The Paranoid Boss

Paranoid people are characterized by systematic delusions and the projection of the conflicts they feel onto others. They are difficult to work with because their perceptions of what is real and what reality is are often not the same. Their mental distortions have become real to them but not to anyone else. Consequently, it is difficult to anticipate, or to defend, their behavior and attitudes. Typical behaviors of paranoid bosses include:

- False accusations of what others are thinking about them
- False interpretations of why others are behaving as they do

Paranoid people have few close colleagues or friends by mutual choice. Their paranoia drives them away from others, and others happily keep their distance, so as to avoid unnecessary conflicts or problems.

Working for a paranoid boss can create a sense of craziness for you. The unrealistic projection of conflict onto others, and possibly onto you, could cause you to consistently assume, defensive posture, making it more difficult to stand out and move ahead.

The On-the-Job Retiree (OJR)

OJR bosses are those who delegate all the work to others, reserving none for themselves. They are active on the payroll, but serve little or no productive function. If they were retired off site, they would hardly be missed—except perhaps at the lunch table.

Knowledgeable about the political structure of the organization, OJRs are proficient at building empires of people to do their work for them, for which they then take full credit. Averse to change or new ideas, the OJR likes to keep things "the way they've always been." It is more comfortable that way, requiring no effort to learn something new.

Somewhat intimidated by overly qualified staff members and high achievers, OJRs tend to surround themselves with mediocrities rather than high-achieving people. They are happy with just enough talent to get the job done.

Their lack of interest in professional progress makes it difficult for their staff to stay abreast of state-of-the-art changes in their profession or industry. And the "easy come, easy go" OJR attitude creates resentment among those who actually do the work but get no credit for it.

OJRs are not likely to be promoted, and they present promotion and advancement blocks for others who work for them.

The Charlie Brown Boss

The Charlie Brown boss is fairly common in business. She exhibits a blend of moods, competencies, and attitudes. Some days are more balanced than others, but by and large she thinks and behaves much as you might expect a boss to, making it easier to talk to her and work with her.

Work performance expectations of subordinates are reasonable, and career development and growth opportunities for subordinates of Charlie Brown supervisors are possible, although not likely to be prominent on the boss's list of priorities unless you bring it to her attention.

The Charlie Brown bosses are approachable and open-minded. Receptive, even encouraging of suggestions for new and better ways of doing the work, they often notice the outstanding performer without further prompting.

Politically astute, but not necessarily heavily involved in office politics, this type of person has a fair chance of earning a promotion. She is well liked by others and creates a cooperative work environment. Overall, a Charlie Brown boss creates a comfortable work environment.

The All-American Boss

For those desirous of career growth and development, the All-American boss profile is the best match. This is the boss whose behavior is grounded in achieving the goals and objectives of the job. Well balanced in attitude, but likely to have high work performance expectations for subordinates, the All-American boss provides opportunities for staff growth, development, and achievement. This type of boss is likely to be extremely busy, but makes time when there is an item of importance.

Abreast of current trends and the latest technology in his field of expertise, the All-American boss is frequently called upon for opinions and advice, and is receptive to and highly encouraging of new ideas.

All-American bosses rely on competent staff members to do their jobs excellently. The dominant goal is to stay on top of the business of being in business. Thus, they recognize and reward outstanding performance. Opportunities to make yourself memorable with All-American bosses are numerous and easy to identify.

The Right Strategy for the Right Boss

It is possible to distinguish yourself in the eyes of each type of boss. The strategy, however, is decidedly different for the different types of boss. Some strategies will feel more comfortable to you than others, depending on your personality, level of self-confidence, and personal values. Strategies that are uncomfortable for you for any reason will not be successful for you. If the prescribed strategy for your boss does not fit well with your skills, personality, or values, then you will probably be better served by exploring alternative employment opportunities where the match between your ability to make yourself memorable and the type of boss you have is more compatible.

Selecting the right strategy depends on the type of boss you have. Some strategies are effective with one type of boss but ineffective with another. Other strategies can be used in combination with one another to create a dual strategy. See Figure 9-2 for a quick reference to the recommended strategy or strategies for each type of boss.

Figure 9-2   The right-boss strategy.

TYPE OF BOSS

		ARROGANT	INCOMPETENT	PARANOID	ON-JOB-RETIREE	CHARLIE BROWN	ALL-AMERICAN
PERFORMANCE STRATEGY	CRUCUAL-SUBORDINATE		√		√	√	√
	PROBLEM-SOLVER	X			√	√	X
	THOUGHT-LEADER		X			√	√
	INFORMATION-RESOURCE		√	√			√
	PUBLIC-RELATIONS	√					

√ = STRONG STRATEGY MATCH TO BOSS TYPE
X = MODERATE MATCH TO BOSS TYPE

There are five primary strategies for making yourself memorable with your boss:

1. Crucial-Subordinate
2. Problem-Solver
3. Thought-Leader
4. Information-Resource
5. Public-Relations

In the following paragraphs we will look at the details of each approach, identify your boss's type, and decide on the strategy that works best with that kind of person.

The principal way of protecting your employment status, of course, is to make yourself indispensable to your boss. When corporate downsizing squeezes are in operation, the indispensable subordinate will be last on the list of prioritized people to be terminated. That is, unless you are indispensable to a boss who has been dispensed with!

To make yourself indispensable, identify the type of boss you have, then study the following strategies identified as effective for your boss type.

The Crucial-Subordinate Strategy

The crucial-subordinate strategy is an effective approach to use with incompetent, OJR, Charlie Brown, and All-American type bosses, but to varying degrees.

The concept of a crucial subordinate, first expressed in the works of Dr. Eugene Jennings, suggests that this subordinate is so needed by the boss that as the boss gets promoted, the subordinate is also promoted, maintaining a continuation of the relationship that was successful before. When Stanley Gault, former president of Rubbermaid Inc., left his previous employer, General Electric, a number of Gault's GE colleagues were recruited to Rubbermaid posts, an example of a crucial-subordinate situation.

The crucial-subordinate strategy is most apt to be successful with All-American and Charlie Brown bosses, who are the most likely types of supervisors to be promoted. Because these two types of managers tend to employ extremely competent people, trusting them to achieve desired goals and objectives with little or no direct involvement by the boss, they are often comfortable developing crucial-subordinate relationships.

Activities or skills that will aid in developing your "crucial" status include:

- Anticipating what the boss needs before it is needed
- Performing technical or support functions that others cannot or do not do as well as you
- Continuing to update your technical skills
- Having strong, honest, and open communication patterns
- Possessing excellent interpersonal skills for smooth communication with the boss as well as representation of the boss in his/her absence
- Exercising visionary skills that are routinely applicable and assist the boss to look good in his/her job
- Using problem-solving skills in crisis situations
- Being always busy and amazingly productive
- Projecting an energized, affirmative attitude
- Reflecting well on the boss who is in direct association with you

In other words, to become a crucial subordinate, fulfill the needs of your boss in such a way that it is perceived that no one can do the job as well as you.

OJR and Incompetent bosses also value the qualities of a crucial subordinate, but only to the extent that they need the centralized competencies they can control and direct in order to keep them from getting into career trouble. Both Incompetent and OJR bosses use the technical skills of a crucial subordinate to do the work that they should be doing but cannot or are unwilling to do. However, such bosses are rarely promoted or rise above their level of incompetence or OJR rank. Therefore, future promotions for you are not probable, and the discovery of their incompetence or nonproductivity could mean career death for this boss, and possibly for you too by virtue of your association with such a person.

Arrogant and Paranoid bosses see little or no value in a crucial subordinate. Arrogant bosses are too self-centered to recognize the talent or value of those who report to them. They function as throwaway people, using the talents of subordinates and then coarsely discarding them when they are no longer needed. And Paranoid bosses are too busy trying to solve the unnecessary problems caused by their paranoia to achieve much progress in their career.

To create your personal crucial-subordinate plan, use the answers to the following questions to prompt the necessary actions:

1. *What skills or talents does the boss need that only I can fill at a superior level of performance?* If the answer to this question is two or fewer skills, you are in trouble, and it is time to identify additional crucial support skills and to begin sharpening your skills in those areas.

2. *What work can I anticipate that the boss will need?* When you have decided, do it in advance, with the finished product ready the moment the assignment is made. Anticipation of work needs and requirements can be done by reviewing your supervisor's upcoming calendar of events. Look at routine tasks, meetings, and reports, and prepare the necessary information in advance in an easy-to-use, professional format.

3. *What work can I do that will make my boss look extraordinary, not just good, in the eyes of others?*

4. What obstacles can get in the way of my becoming the crucial subordinate?

When your answers to these questions are complete, review your current behavior in the light of what is needed to become a crucial subordinate and prioritize the necessary actions.

The Problem-Solver Strategy

The problem-solver strategy is most effective with OJR and Charlie Brown type bosses. The concept of the problem-solver strategy suggests that competent and creative individuals can pull together solutions to any number of problems or difficulties that the boss may encounter. These people become known as problem solvers.

Typically optimistic, creative in nature, resourceful in approach, skillful in negotiating and human relations, competent in general engineering, and unbridled in their thinking, problem-solving individuals consistently find acceptable solutions to difficult, problem-laden situations.

For OJR and Charlie Brown bosses, the problem solver is essential to their sanity. In the case of OJRs, problem solvers are essential to their continued employment because they provide the solutions to daily operating challenges. Often the ability of OJRs to visualize solutions is limited by their personal lack of initiative.

On the other hand, Charlie Brown bosses value the work of problem solvers, recognizing the contribution of their skills to the overall achievement of goals, and as being in their own best interests. In essence, the Charlie Brown boss highly values a combination of crucial-subordinate and problem-solver strategies, whereas the OJR boss sees value only in the problem solver.

Arrogant and All-American type bosses view problem solving in a helpful, positive way, but of lesser importance or value than other strategies, such as the crucial-subordinate strategy.

Arrogant bosses value anything you do to make them look better in the eyes of others or to bolster their self-initiated image of importance. But however accepting of your solutions and contributions they may be, they are frequently not appreciative of them. And as much as the All-American bosses value the assistance provided by a problem solver, they are not overly consumed with an affinity for that skill.

To become memorable as a problem solver, you must display consistency of attitude and results. The complexity, scope, and frequency of problems solved distinguishes a memorable problem solver from a periodic problem solver. The more complex the problem, the more memorable the solution will be, and the more memorable the person associated with finding that solution becomes. The broader the scope of the problem, the more memorable the solution will be. The more frequently problems are resolved, the more memorable you become as a problem solver.

The problem-solving strategy is particularly effective when used in combination with the crucial subordinate strategy or the thought-leader strategy, which, as a package, comprises both extremes; the ability to think of new ideas, and the ability to find ways to implement them.

Use the following questions and ideas to develop your personal action plan for becoming a memorable problem solver: .

1. *Identify current boss-plaguing problems.* Get involved in resolving them. Choose problems that others are not addressing, and personally address them. When building your initial image as a problem solver, the state of simplicity or sophistication of the problem is not as important as the gross number of problems that you can resolve in a short time. Initially build up the volume of problems solved in order to create your image, then move on to more sophisticated and complex problems.

2. *Promote results.* Once the problem is resolved, bring forth a summary of the problems and the solutions that you personally put into place. Bombard your boss with a long list of impressive results that demonstrate your skills as a problem solver.

3. *Get aggressive.* Ask to be included in more difficult, broader-scope problems that are currently under consideration.

It's never too late to join a problem-solving team. Be vocal and bold in your attack on problems.

The Thought-Leader Strategy

The thought-leader strategy is highly valued by the All-American, Charlie Brown, and Incompetent types of bosses, but is not so valued by Arrogant, Paranoid, and OJR bosses. The concept of the thought leader has its roots in the need for being competitive to survive. Organizations and people with breakthrough ideas and approaches are considered to be thought leaders, and it is this thought-leading quality that gives them a distinctive competitive advantage over others. Thought leaders are visionary, creative individuals who develop the breakthrough ideas that shape the future.

All-American and Charlie Brown bosses respect and highly value the contribution of thought leaders to the overall achievement of their goals. They look to thought leaders to provide them with the cutting-edge thinking that will make them memorable to their targeted audiences.

Arrogant, know-it-all bosses, convinced that no one knows better than they do, see little value in thought leaders. They may even view thought leaders as a threat.

OJR bosses are too lazy to do anything with ideas brought forth by new thinking. They'd rather not be bothered. And the twisted thinking of Paranoid bosses makes deciphering breakthrough thinking too difficult for them.

The thought-leading approach is most powerful and effective when combined with the problem-solver strategy or the crucial-subordinate strategy. The combined set of skills represents the ability to conceive and the ability to implement a powerful and valued package. For example, business planning cannot occur without the thought leader, who provides the vision or direction for the future. Nor can it be successful without the problem solver, who will make the thought leader's vision a reality. And the crucial subordinate is key in implementing the final design.

Intellectually based, thought leaders, like visionaries, spin current known facts into the future, envisioning what the continuing evolution of facts and of certain combinations of facts will mean. To sharpen your thought-leader skills, consider the following three exercises:

1. *Read, read, read.* Read everything and anything you can get your hands on related to the topics and issues that your boss and business are concerned with. Reading will broaden your base of knowledge.
2. *Listen.* Listen to what other leaders in the industry are saying and to what industry strategists are projecting. Integrate what you read with what you hear. Where are there incongruities? Where are there similar themes?
3. *Converse and brainstorm.* Engage in creative, no-holds-barred thinking with colleagues and others whose opinions are respected. Consider their brainstorming comments and ideas seriously. Could any of this thinking lead to new approaches?

The Information-Resource Strategy

The information-resource strategy is based on the concept that he who has the knowledge has the power. Information-resource people have access to a full range of valued information including:

- What's on the grapevine
- What's in the business computer
- What key operative people are thinking or talking about
- What competitors are talking about or doing

The information-resource strategy is highly valued by Paranoid and Incompetent boss types. Paranoid bosses, more than any other boss types, need a frequent feed of information in order to correct their twisted thinking and to dilute the paranoia they continually create.

Incompetent bosses value information as a means of keeping themselves out of trouble. If the information feed is accurate and fast enough, an Incompetent boss gains the time to cover for weaknesses or errors before they are detected by anyone in authority.

The risk of the information approach is that your value to your boss then becomes a direct reflection of the quality of the information provided. If the information is accurate and hard to come by, you will be highly valued and indispensable. If the information is inaccurate or simply common knowledge, you will be considered dispensable.

To implement an information-resource strategy, you need to be comfortable in the company of gossip. Get plugged into the company, executive, and community grapevines. Not everyone will be accepted in all these closed communities. And if accepted, you then need to get comfortable with the idea of sharing what is learned from these sources with your boss.

The Public-Relations Strategy

The concept of the public relations strategy is that of generating internal and external interest in a specific person or event, of creating a sense of importance that directly feeds into the single most intense need of Arrogant bosses—to be seen and viewed as important, as more important than they actually are.

People who can effectively create or enhance the image of their boss, particularly an Arrogant boss, will be held in high regard by that person. Because arrogance is a difficult quality to live with, few people are willing to work to enhance what is already a trying attitude. However, if this is your boss type, this is very likely the most direct and effective means of making yourself memorable with him.

To create a public-relations strategy action plan that will be effective in making yourself memorable to your boss—and still make working with an arrogant supervisor tolerable—follow these prescriptions:

1. *Become a private coach.* In privacy, coach your boss on how to manage the damaging behaviors that result from his arrogant attitude. You can broach the topic with such introductory statements as, "You probably are unaware of the way these actions are being perceived." Or, "because I've had the opportunity to get to know you, I know that the way you're being perceived is different from the way you really are, or different from the way

you want to be thought of." To the extent that the arrogant supervisor is desirous of improving his relationships, he will value your coaching, and perhaps take you into his confidence, which is an indication that you are becoming more important to him. To the extent that the arrogance is out of control, there is nothing more you can do to make yourself either memorable or indispensable.

2. *Build a PR machine.* Identify and create opportunities for your boss to be profiled by corporate and community leaders and organizations. Nominate him for awards and support him in his efforts to compete for recognition—all the while coaching him on more acceptable ways of displaying his arrogance.

Rules for Every Employment Relationship

The following set of employment behaviors, by setting you apart from the crowd, will make you memorable to your boss.

Achieving Peak Performance

1. Anticipate needs.
2. Demonstrate high quality immediately.
3. Know the work rules and follow them.
4. Go beyond your job by doing far more than whatever is expected.
5. Avoid making excuses.
6. Implement your new ideas for improvement.
7. Make the boss look extraordinary to others.
8. Grow the system.
9. Pick your battles carefully.
10. Look as if you're contributing.
11. Follow up on all your efforts.
12. Don't challenge the boss, challenge the system.
13. Do what the boss wants.
14. Create opportunities for self-exposure.
15. Be bold in your comments and opinions.
16. Enjoy!

Building Strong Relationships

1. Make impressions for the long term.
2. Be loyal.
3. Be committed and show it.
4. Fight nonsense.
5. Be honest.
6. In private, share information that others will not.
7. Use common sense.
8. Don't compromise on your principles.
9. Make it easy for others to assist or participate in your initiatives.
10. Play the game to win.

Things to Worry About With Your Boss

There are some things that people tend to worry about but shouldn't. And there are other things worth worrying about. In the effort to make yourself memorable to your boss, the following questions are worth your time and concern:

1. *What new work is the boss doing that I can do for him?* Taking on something extra relieves the boss of part of his work load and simultaneously develops your skills and the scope of your job.
2. *What should I anticipate next?* Is there a crisis that can be headed off? Or one that you can resolve?
3. What can I do to make my boss look significantly better to peers and superiors?
4. *How highly is the work I do valued by my boss?* How can that opinion be improved upon further?
5. *When was the last time I made an appreciable contribution?* If it's been longer than thirty days, it's time to become innovative and imaginative and make another significant contribution.
6. *What have I done in the last thirty days to make myself noticeable?*
7. Am I being bold enough?
8. Am I creating enough opportunities for myself to become memorable?

Things Not to Worry About With Your Boss

The following are things that are not worth your time or worry because they will not affect you over the long term:

1. *Do others like me?* Your job is not a popularity contest. The only thing that matters is if your boss likes you.
2. *Are people talking about me?* Get used to it. People talk about notable people, and you are distinguishing yourself from the crowd, making yourself a notable person.
3. *Why are little personal requests being made of me?* Don't be judgmental about the value of small personal tasks that your boss may ask you to do. As your relationship grows, small favors go both ways, more out of a sense of friendship and teamwork than out of the supervisor/ subordinate relationship.

10

Make Yourself
Memorable to Family
and Friends

"Relationships are the best part of life."
—Stephanie Sherman

Family relationships are the first and the most enduring relationships in our lives. Mother and child bonding begins as early as the moment of birth. Some claim that it begins even earlier, in the womb. Family members provide relationships that last in one form or another from the cradle to the grave, struggling through challenging times and celebrating happier times. Some even say that relationships exist after death. In the movie *I Never Sang for My Father*, actor Gene Hackman says, "Death may end a life, but it doesn't end a relationship."

Unfortunately, today's life-styles often do not allow for adequate family development. Two-career families, nontraditional home structures, unemployment, and social distractions all contribute to weak family entities. Often, little more than communal living among related people results, lessening and diluting the value of family relationships.

How can we build memorable and valued family relationships? How can family relationships be restored to their original luster and importance?

Family relationships are, and should be, different from other relationships. They are more intense in nature, longer-lasting, and larger in scope. By understanding the cornerstone behaviors that create memorable family relationships, you can develop and fortify the particular behaviors that contribute to revitalizing the quality of your family life.

Numerous characteristics contribute to making memorable family relationships, but five particular characteristics serve as the foundation upon which memorable and lasting relationships can be built (see Figure 10-1). Use these five characteristics to create vibrant and memorable family relations.

Four of these characteristics—love, honesty, dependability, and generosity—define the parameters and types of behaviors that build memorable one-on-one relationships among family members. The fifth characteristic, identity, is not an individual behavior but rather the sense of belonging to a unique entity that all family members feel.

The following sections define each characteristic and provide prescriptions that can be immediately put to use toward creating memorable relationships.

Love and Acceptance

Love is the most universal characteristic of memorable family relationships. For our purposes, love is defined as the unconditional acceptance of a person. Regardless of how someone looks or acts, or who they become, love means always and unconditionally accepting that family member. Ellen Goodman said it well: "We don't have to achieve to be accepted by our family. We

Figure 10-1   Five family cornerstones.

- **LOVE & ACCEPTANCE**
- **HONESTY & TRUST**
- **DEPENDABILITY**
- **GENEROSITY**
- **IDENTITY**

just have to be." Relationships void of love cannot mature to a highly memorable status.

There are many ways of expressing love for another person. Most expressions of love can be summarized under five fundamental categories of behavior. These five behaviors are:

1. Showing concern
2. Taking an interest
3. Touching
4. Expressing caring words
5. Giving special attention

The application and execution of each behavior must be individually created and uniquely delivered. The critical factor is that the intended message be received for what it is meant to be.

The following suggested behaviors will help you deliver your message of love.

1. *Showing concern.* Often we feel concern for another, but do not know how to express it. One effective way to express concern is to ask questions, listen to the answers, and then act. Sensitive inquiries, active listening, and responsive actions will show your concern. The following questions begin the process of asking, listening, and acting:

"How are you doing?"
"What can I do to help?"
"What do you need?"
"I'd like to assist in some way."
"Tell me what you're thinking."

2. *Taking an interest.* "How is it going?" "I've been thinking about you," "I'd like to get involved with..." or "Tell me about..." are starters for expressing your interest. In addition to these verbal approaches, you can also try activity-based approaches as a more tangible means of expressing your interest. Get involved in activities that are important in the life of the other, even if your participation is passive.

For instance, attend your son's Little League games or your daughter's debut in the annual high school play. If your husband or wife is chairperson of the town fund-raising drive, demonstrate your interest by volunteering to help out. Identify whatever areas interest the person you are "targeting" and find ways to participate in those areas of interest. Become involved in as many areas of interest as possible. The more areas of interest you become involved in, or the more significant your involvement is, the more memorable it is likely to be.

3. *Touching.* People are tactile and sensitive to touch. Much can be communicated through a single touch. Types of communicative touching that convey caring to the other person include:

- Holding hands
- Placing a hand on the other's shoulder
- Giving a rub around the neck
- Hugging
- Affectionately squeezing
- Tickling

Touching is one expression of love that is universally understood, if not always explainable.

4. *Expressing caring words.* Words of love need to be spoken many times daily to those we care for. Such words never wear thin or grow old. Be generous in their use. Ways to verbally express caring include these statements:

"You mean the world to me."
"You are important to me."
"You are special to me."
"I care for you."
"I think you are wonderful."

Set yourself the goal of sending a caring message at least three times a day to those you love. Morning, noon, and night. You can play a little game each morning to see who will be first to say "I love you." The game format is a reminder to verbally share what you are feeling. The impact can be amazing.

5. *Giving special attention.* Special attention is a demonstrated interest in some activity or aspect of another that goes beyond routine, normal attention levels. Depending on the interests and needs of the other person, special attention can be

demonstrated in an infinite number of ways. Some things you can do to provide special attention are:

- *Draw attention to the other person.* Admirable qualities, behaviors, incidents, and achievements are rallying points for the attention of others. The dinner table is a natural setting at which to draw the attention of family members, but don't limit attention giving to meal-times. Use any opportunity that arises. For example, while waiting in a bank line with my son Adam, my arm draped around his shoulder, I turned to the stranger behind me and said, "Isn't he a handsome young man?" The attention focused on Adam for a moment. Embarrassed on the outside, yet flattered on the inside, Adam blushed and turned, knowing that I thought he was "special."

- *Set time aside.* The most precious and irretrievable of all commodities is time. Therefore, a gift of time to some-one is another way of saying, "You're special to me. I'd rather spend time with you now than be anywhere else." Set aside a block of time daily to spend with those in whom you want to generate a greater feeling of love. How often have you heard people describe some mem-orable person in their life as "acting as though he had all the time in the world for me." The more time you give, the more important the other will feel.

- *Give the gift of self.* Within your pile of material posses-sions, large or small, choose an item that has a special connection to you, and will also have a special mean-ing to the recipient. Give it as a "gift of self." The "self" is the connection to you. Items linked to a personal story shared between the two of you will be most memorable. To create the most memorable impression, explain why you are giving the gift, how special the person is to be chosen to receive the gift, what the con-nection means to you, and what the history of the object is that makes it an appropriate gift.

- *Participate in a special event.* Participate in activities cho-sen by the other—things that you have never before done together. Let that person set the agenda; then show up ready to go. Temporarily move into your child's or your spouse's world by actively participating in their interests in which you've never, or only rarely, participated in the past. Get on that bicycle and spend the afternoon with your children. Play house with younger children. Go hiking with teenage children. Go fishing with your husband. Go shopping with your wife. Act and look interested and energized!

- *Make a sacrifice.* Give up something you want to do, or have planned to do, in the interest of spending time with another. Or give up something you desire for yourself in exchange for giving something of importance to another. Oseola McCarty, as reported in the *Chicago Tribune,* is a touching example of sacrifice. Scrimping throughout her life and saving what she earned from doing laundry for others, she finally retired at age 87. In retirement she donated the amazing sum of $150,000 to the local university to fund higher education for deserving young people, youngsters with talent and potential but no opportunity for formal education. Throughout her long life she had lived frugally in order to give something of great value to others.*

What can you sacrifice in order to give to others? Choose one item or activity each month that you can sacrifice. Donate the money or time saved to an activity that will make a memorable occasion or help build a desired relationship. Explain what you are doing to those who will benefit from your sacrifice. When they understand the source and depth of the giving, the gift will be more memorable.

Honesty and Trust

Honesty is the quality that allows a relationship to grow; it is the nurturing and fostering quality of a relationship. Honesty separates what is real from what is not. A less than honest individual creates an artificial, shallow, and limited relationship beyond which memories cannot penetrate.

*Chicago Tribune, August 5, 1995.

To foster honesty among family members consider the following ideas:

1. *Give recognition, reinforcement, and rewards for honesty.* Honesty in tough matters deserves special recognition. When the price of honesty is high, the recognition and reward should also be high. Draw attention to situations where honest behavior stands out. Publicly recognize and reward the desired behavior.

2. *Be a role model where honesty is concerned.* Teach by your example. Every aspect of your behavior must display honesty. Point out situations where dishonest opportunities presented themselves, and explain why you chose honesty. Then celebrate the chosen behavior.

3. *Teach honesty.* Teach through practice opportunities. Create situations where dishonesty could be a choice. When honesty prevails, award praise, hugs, reinforcement, and fun. When dishonesty is chosen, correct the thinking that lies behind the choice. Create a family "Honest to Pete" award (insert the individual's name in place of "Pete") to be given to family members when they exhibit extraordinary honesty in difficult situations. Give it liberally and frequently. With this award should come some special privilege otherwise unavailable—a reward for honest behavior.

Dependability

Dependability is a first cousin to reliability and trust, the basic elements of relationships that endure. Confucius says, "A man who lacks reliability is utterly useless."

Being reliable in one's behavior and attitude creates dependability; others can trust that these qualities will always be there and can therefore depend on the person having them. Without reliability, dependability is impossible. And the greater the sense of dependability, the more memorable the relationship is likely to be. Lack of dependability creates apprehensiveness, a barrier to relationship growth.

To foster dependability among individual family members, consider these approaches:

1. *Serve as a role model for dependability.* Teach by personal example. Point out the number of situations where others

depend on you to do something for them. Create a visual representation of the amount of interrelational dependency that exists among family members by using pennies and a bowl as symbolic props. Each time a family member recognizes that another family member is doing something for them that they are dependent on, have them put a penny in the bowl. Examples of parental behavior upon which children and others depend include the provision of food, shelter, clothing, transportation, and assistance with schoolwork, to name just the major items. Children demonstrate their dependability through being on time so that others do not have to wait and by following through on what they say they will do. The bowl of pennies will quickly fill up, demonstrating that there is a great need for dependability in family relationships.

Personalize this exercise for each child by providing each one with a bowl and pennies. How much dependability are various family members providing for one another? Coach and counsel those who are demonstrating less than the desired levels of dependability, and reward those exhibiting unusual levels of dependability. Make it a fun game that teaches and motivates dependable behavior.

2. *Teach through experience.* Assign family members responsibilities tied to a desired result whose success depends on each doing his or her share as part of a team. Celebrate when the result is achieved. The achievement and celebration of goals reinforce the desired behavior of dependability, which, over the long run, becomes a personal quality in each family member that makes the relationship memorable. Take failed situations and use them to teach and coach, repeating your efforts until they succeed.

3. *Recognize, reinforce, and reward dependable behavior.* Seek out examples of extraordinarily dependable behavior displayed by family members, and make heroes of those who demonstrate this quality. Tell their story of dependability in slow, painstaking detail, reinforcing them for every action. Finally, present an award—something that otherwise would not have been available to them or permitted them. Directly tie the award to the dependability behavior, emphasizing its importance.

At work, one hospital created "Caught in the Act" coupons. Associates give them to each other when a person is "caught in the act" of providing real service, quality, or teamwork. The coupon is good for meals in the cafeteria and also makes recipients eligible for a larger prize in a raffle drawing.

Name your award something that relates to the dependability experience in order to retain the connection between the idea of dependability, the actual experience, and the reward for it. By naming each award, it is easier to recollect and to refer to the situation in conversations.

Generosity

Generosity, as defined by the dictionary, is a "readiness or liberality of giving." First cousin to sharing, generosity connotes *giving beyond what is expected*. When the reality of a gift is greater than our expectations, we think of it as generous.

Some level of generosity is already evident in your family environment. It is commonly evidenced in the form of parents giving generously to their children—giving of their time, sacrificing luxury, leisure, and desirable items for the sake of what the children want or need. However, sometimes generosity is misinterpreted by the receiver as something owed, as an entitlement. There is a difference between giving or providing something to a child or others out a sense of responsibility and giving or providing at a generous level. The difference is in the volume of what is given or the intensity of the giving, as well as in the total resources from which it is given. Generosity is giving above and beyond what is expected or what is fundamentally needed.

Building generous behavior in families is a two-pronged task. First, family members need to understand what generosity is and how to identify it in other family members. Second, generosity needs to be demonstrated in uncommon as well as common ways in order for it to become memorable. Uncommon acts of generosity draw on the memory-making strategy of "unexpected events" and the M factor of "sharing" to build a memorable image.

Learning Generosity

Some people are naturally generous, while others have to learn how to behave in a generous way. Once identified, acts of generosity serve as models for further acts of generosity. The following ideas will help family members learn how to identify acts of generosity among themselves.

1. *Keep a family chart of generosity.* The idea behind charting generosity levels is to identify the gross amount of generosity currently being shown among family members, to counsel and coach those who need to learn more generosity, and to reward those individuals when they have learned and applied this behavior. The process for charting generosity starts with a *Family Chart of Generous Deeds* posted on your refrigerator door or in some other common location. Each time a family member experiences an act of generosity from another family member, make a mark on the family chart. The goal is to build the number of generous family acts from one week to the next. At the end of each week, discuss the extent of generosity displayed as evidenced on the chart and set new goals for the following period. Soon, acts of generosity will become a normal part of your family interactions.

2. *Set generosity goals.* Generosity goals for one family member can be different in size and scope than for another member, depending on the ages of the people involved. Young children are capable of demonstrating frequency of generosity; however, the scope of their generosity will be smaller. For example, children can be taught that sharing toys is an act of generosity to be frequently demonstrated. Older children can demonstrate a broader scope of generosity by sharing favorite clothes, accessories, and bigger toys, as well as by being generous with their time, their willingness to do household chores, and to lend assistance to others.

Some level of generosity currently exists within your family. The goal is to expand that level until frequent acts of generosity become second nature to all family members. One fun way is to use the *Family Chart of Generous Deeds.* As a family, review the current level of family generosity and decide on a new goal two or three times greater. When the goal is reached, a significant celebration is needed—perhaps a family vacation, or outing.

3. *Reward, recognize, and reinforce acts of generosity.* New behavior requires reinforcement in the shape of a reward for it to be repeated. When the new level of behavior is achieved, a small celebration is called for. Amusing and semivaluable rewards keep such celebrations interesting.

Consider establishing categories of "extreme" generosity behavior. "Extreme" is an excellent category to select because it is one of the strongest M factors for making yourself memorable. Thus, while teaching the concepts of generosity, you can also be creating memorable experiences for family members—a double-win situation. Ideas for categories of generosity to be awarded include:

- The Most Generous Act
- The Most Outrageous Act of Generosity
- The Greatest Volume of Generous Acts
- The Most Difficult Act of Generosity

All family members should receive some kind of recognition for the generosity they have displayed.

Random Acts of Generosity

Random acts of generosity are sometimes the most memorable. Because generosity is based on giving, gifts of nearly any nature should be interpreted as generous. However, gifts of intangibles are often especially memorable because they are less common and require more creativity.

Use the successfully proven ideas on this list, or generate new ideas, for both demonstrating your generosity and creating a memorable moment.

1. *Give dedications.* Dedications are a way of giving an intangible as a gift. Anything can be dedicated to anyone and made a memorable event. Things you can dedicate include:

- This day's work
- A prayer
- A song on the radio, followed up by a copy of the song
- A poem—one you wrote yourself or are particularly fond of
- A meal
- A favorite or secret recipe
- An achievement goal, for example,
  —Winning a game
  —Getting good grades

—Graduating from a class
—Getting a promotion
- A tree or flower bed
- A building, bridge, room, road, or woodland trail
- An effort, for example,
—A tournament
—A contribution to a worthy cause
—A moment of silence
—A well-intended wish

2. *Give time.* Time is the only irretrievable asset that dissipates at a constant rate. A gift of time is the most valuable gift of all. Some ideas of how the gift of time can be used include:

- Time to talk—Uninterrupted, one-on-one talking about whatever the other person wants to talk about
- Time to help with the chores that another is responsible for
- Time to be together with a sick person—even in silence
- Time to help with another person's problem
- Time to listen when someone wants to tell you something
- Time to do something extra, unexpected, and unasked for
- Time that was reserved for yourself

3. *Exceed expectations.* Give more than what is needed or asked for. Splurge. Here are some ideas to get you thinking in the right channels.

- If you're taking the kids on an outing, take along a friend of theirs, perhaps someone less privileged.
- Buy the big box of popcorn.
- Buy the earrings that go with the necklace.
- Make the dessert from scratch, not from a ready mix.
- Pack "special treats" for traveling family members.

In general,
- Arrive earlier.
- Stay longer.
- Listen longer.

- Give more.
- Buy bigger.
- Bring more.
- Do the undone.

4. *Sacrifice.* All aspects of giving involve a sacrifice of some kind. The concept of sacrifice to make yourself memorable is a concept greater than giving. It means giving at the personal expense of losing something for yourself, of forgoing something in order to give to another—an extremely powerful way in which to make yourself memorable.

Because sacrifice is a significant act, the number and extent of sacrifices that any one person can make is limited. Carefully choose those people and events you are willing to sacrifice for. To make your gift of sacrifice memorable, others need to know what sacrifice was made. Without knowing that a sacrifice was involved, the true value of the gift of generosity is never entirely known.

What Constitutes a Memorable Sacrifice?

A sacrifice is made whenever something of value and importance to you is forgone in exchange for the opportunity to give to someone else. The key words are *value* and *importance*. If it is not of value or important to you, it may be a gift, but it is not a sacrifice.

Sacrifices become particularly memorable when they are unexpected and highly valued by the recipient. The greater the sacrifice, and the more unexpected the event, the more memorable it may become.

Answers to the following four questions will help you to assess potential items or behaviors that would qualify as a memorable sacrifice.

1. What do family members need that they cannot acquire through their own resources? How important a need do they perceive this to be?
2. What sacrifice can you make to help them satisfy their need?
3. Is this a sacrifice you are willing to make?
4. If the sacrifice is made, will it make a significant difference for the other person?

Identity

The Old Testament proverb says, "Remove not the ancient land-mark, which the fathers have set." Identity of self and family are integral to building and retaining a memorable family. "Who am I?" "Where did I come from?": These are the questions we must be able to answer to feel whole. Yet our heritage—and thus an important part of our personal identity—is often neglected and unnurtured. Fostering family identity serves as a source of pride and helps us to bond with other family members. It provides a meaningful rationale for long-held family traditions.

A strong sense of family identity is a source of emotional strength. We feel pride in the achievements of our ancestors and relate to events of the past that help define who we are today.

Supporting and bolstering family identity is one way of honoring current family members by way of paying our respects to those who have gone before. In the past, strong ethnic societies preserved their traditions, thus enhancing an understanding of the value of family heritage. However, the great American melting pot is rapidly diluting the distinguishing nature of these different heritages.

There are several ways to rebuild family identity and to strengthen the bonds among family members:

1. *Research your family's genealogy.* What does the family tree look like? What interesting tidbits can be discovered about people on the tree? Are there any members of royalty, celebrities, heroes, or villains among your ancesters? The local library can provide a start in terms of resources and contact points for genealogical research. Share the results of your research with all family members. Paint a visual picture of who these people were, how they lived, and what their life trials and achievements were.

2. *Research family symbols.* Incorporate the heraldic family symbol or any other symbol of family identity into as many aspects of family life as possible. Put it on your house sign, personal stationery, Christmas cards, name tags, customized pottery, invitations, T-shirts, or any other item you think

appropriate. Use it as a family signature where you would normally print your name and address. Frequent exposures to the family symbol reinforce the sense of family identity.

3. *Sponsor family reunions.* Geographic distance sometimes equates to fading relationships and memories. Family reunions bring people together, revitalizing faded memories and renewing our acquaintance with distant relatives. It is a time for information gathering and for strengthening the sense of identity in an extended family.

4. *Build and protect family traditions.* Build on whatever traditions are in place by improving on them. Create new traditions—holiday traditions, relationship traditions, daily traditions. Encourage each family member to create one new tradition for the entire family to carry out. For example, our family tradition each Fourth of July is to salute and fly the American flag, say the Pledge of Allegiance, and kiss the ground beneath the flag to demonstrate our respect and thankfulness for a free country.

5. *Publish a family newsletter.* Communication is the link keeping us in touch with one another, keeping relationships alive. A family newsletter is a way of sharing triumphs and tragedies with all the family. By sharing family information, family newsletters document the lives of family members who are geographically dispersed, yet somehow emotionally connected. Include photos, updates on achievements, career changes, family plans, vacations, hopes, wishes, dreams, and personal messages.

6. *Go camping.* Camping is a bonding experience that is difficult to explain. People who have gone camping know the special relationships that develop in a natural, noncommercialized environment. There is something about being close to nature, removed from routine distractions and dependent on one another for survival, that brings out personal qualities otherwise unknown. This is a type of intimacy shared only among the campers.

7. *Monogram.* Monograms are an abbreviated version of your name. Wearing a monogram is a sign of family pride. Monogram everything within reason. Consider monogramming the following items:

Personal Items

- Shirts and blouses
- Scarfs and handkerchiefs
- Tie pins and cuff links
- Lapel pins

- Earrings
- Charms

- Rings
- Money clips
- Briefcases
- Wallets and accessory carriers
- Desk accessories

Family Items

- Crystal or glassware
- Family silverware
- Linens—table napkins, bed sheets, pillow cases, towels
- Luggage or handbag
- Sidewalk in front of your house
- Welcome mat
- Photo frames and photo album covers
- Trivets
- Wall hangings

8. *Inscribe everything.* Anything that can be inscribed should be—books, cards, photos, jewelry, art, stories, awards, and correspondence of any kind. Inscriptions are a way of tying yourself and your sentiments eternally to the gift. Some old books were found in the attic. They were inscribed to "Clayton with love, Mother," and dated fifty years ago. This is a keepsake for Clayton and the family that comes after him. A piece of "Mother" lives on in her inscription. It is a way of keeping a memory alive.

9. *Keep a family scrapbook.* A source of identity for those who come after us, the family scrapbook should be filled with pieces of our lives, both current and past. These include photos, articles, stories of family members, proofs of achievement, important letters, birth certificates, marriage certificates, the deed to the first house, locks of hair, baby's first fingerprints and footprints. Anything and everything that is connected to the present family will someday become part of our memories. Scrapbooks serve not only as documented histories of the family but also as orientation pieces for new family members. Share them with fiancés and children when they come of age.

"Working the Magic" of Family Relationships

I thank my son Jonathan for the phrase "working the magic." Often he asks if I will be working the magic, meaning, will I be doing something that will make another person feel special, creating a magical transformation or feeling.

The magic of any relationship is that which makes the other feel special. To feel that we are important is a universal desire we all share. Working the magic is the idea of planning special events or activities that result in making someone else feel special—a magical transformation from feeling ordinary to the feeling of uncommon well-being. It is easy to do.

Magic-Making Moms

Moms are magical people. The giving of birth is in itself magical. From that very first moment, moms continue to make magic daily for the family. If you're a mom wanting to make yourself magically memorable to those you love, consider the following advice and prescriptions.

1. *Revisit good advice.* Frequently revisit the good advice provided by Thomas Jefferson to his daughter Martha, and by me to you: "Be you, my dear, the link of love, union and peace for the whole family." The sum of your memory-making behaviors are in this advice.

2. *Give comfort and support.* There are times and events in life when the comfort and support provided by mom seem magical. No one can do it the way she does! For example, when you are down with a bout of the flu, mom's comfort, hugs, and special soup are important ingredients in the healing process. Or when trouble comes your way, mom's support and attention to the matter seem to soothe the situation. Comfort and support are ageless, magical bonding behaviors that are especially potent when they come from mom. As a mom yourself, be there, regardless, when comfort and support are most needed.

3. *Applaud.* Applause is the motivating fuel for more and greater performances in one's life. Magical moms act as chief lifelong cheerleaders, applauding loudest and longest for the efforts of their children. To make yourself memorable, become a

chief cheerleader for every member of the family, cheering long and loud for even the smallest achievements of others.

4. *Be a caretaker.* Broad in scope, caretaking refers to overseeing the needs of others—from their practical daily living needs to fragile spiritual needs. The magic is that mom can do so much, and at the exact moment it is needed. Identify the unfulfilled needs of family members, and strategize how you can fill them in part or in full.

5. *Show understanding.* Magical moms have an uncanny ability to understand both the routine and the more obscure feelings and situations of others. A natural bonding occurs between people who understand one another. Because moms often spend more individual time with family members by virtue of their "mom role," they are often more able to be understanding.

To create that magical feeling that results from understanding, use the contrarian factor, choosing an extreme situation where little understanding seems to exist between one family member and the others. Express your solid and unwavering understanding of the person in the minority, even though you may not be thoroughly familiar with the details of the situation. This will generate a feeling of oneness with you. The concerns and problems that children must deal with today are dramatically different from those that previous generations faced; thus it will likely take some time for you to come up to speed on their issues. When you provide an island of understanding in a sea of misunderstanding, you will become memorable.

6. *Use your talents.* Identify something you can do better than any other mom you know—or something you can do that constitutes an important skill or talent in the eyes of your child, and use it to advance your position of importance. The talent or skill viewed as important by your child will change over time as he or she grows and changes. Build your repertoire of talents, continuing to hone your past skills while simultaneously adding a new generation of skills and building a memorable history of things you did "just for the fun of it."

Undistracted Dads

Undistracted dads are those who fend off the self-serving distractions of life to focus on the development of strong interactive family relationships. Sometimes at a disadvantage, dads have fewer natural opportunities for family interaction. The historical role of dad as family hunter and protector frequently pulled him away from the family, leaving little time for relationship development. Undistracted dads focus their time and efforts on specific memory-making activities and values.

To make yourself memorable, consider these winning techniques:

1. *Clear your calendar.* Choose one or two school activities and one or two extracurricular activities, then clear your calendar so you can attend. Don't let distractions get in the way. Make whatever sacrifices are necessary. When sacrifices are called for, let others know that you are making the sacrifice for them. This will create an image of dependability, and make the other feel special.

2. *Stick to the deal.* When you say you're going to do something, do it. We frequently underestimate the damage a broken promise can do. A promise broken is more than a broken promise; it can shatter a child's sense of security.

3. *Focus on them.* Participation and involvement in all aspects of their lives are important to children. Go to extremes to get involved. As school projects are assigned, partner with your child to create the best darned project in the class. Build a sense of pride in the team effort and at the same time create a bonding and memorable experience. The more frequently you interact with your kids, the more likely you are to become memorable to them. Children must see that you love them. Suggested starting points to boost your image to new heights include:

- Take them for their "firsts." The "first" driving lesson, the "first" lawn tractor ride, the "first" athletic supporter purchase, the "first" barber shop visit, the "first" shaving experience—for boys, at any rate. Make a list of other "firsts" that you can plan to be a part of.
- Participate in school field trips and other unique experiences.
- Keep a sense of humor and display it frequently.
- Wrestle with the boys on the family room floor.
- Tickle the kids until they cry tears of laughter.

- Talk with them personally about the daily events of their lives. Give kind guidance. Dad talk is different from mom talk, and both are needed.
- Rent a bicycle built for two.
- Stand up for them, no matter what the situation.
- Take them out for lunch occasionally.
- Introduce them to the machinery of life—engines, power tools, automobiles, and the like.
- Take them to work with you.
- Designate a family night each week dedicated to family activities.
- Offer solutions to their problems, but don't push your solutions on them.
- Be generous with compliments.
- Be generous with encouragement.
- Create a family theater in your living room, with everybody playing a role in this homemade production.
- Create your own special "good night" saying. "Good night, I love you, see you in the morning," says it all at our house.
- Put a note in your child's lunch box.
- Paint a rock in the yard with the child's name on it.
- Always have a small surprise on hand, such as their favorite candy, comic book, or game.
- Be there to provide support regardless of the cause.

4. *Support family values.* Family values represent the core beliefs in accordance with which decisions are made and behavior is judged as appropriate or not. Be clear, focused, and unwavering in your support of family values, and exemplify a standard of behavior upon which all other family members can rely. Create a family values statement.

Undistracted dads balance the role of family provider and protector with the personal relationship-building needs of others by focusing their time and activities on memory-making moments. "It is the great man who does not lose his child's heart," says Menicius. How many meanings do you see in this piece of philosophical wisdom?

Spouse Spice: Making Yourself Memorable to Your Spouse

Individual life experiences and long-held hopes and dreams often serve as the source for great memory-making ideas. At other times, spontaneous, wildly "not you," zany and uncensored behavior becomes eternally memorable. Still other memories stem from a sequence of wonderfully sensitive and loving experiences.

The following lists of things to try could spark a special memorable experience for your spouse:

Adventureland

1. Arrange for a hot-air balloon ride. Up, up, and away!
2. Arrange for a para-sailing ride. Up, up, and away over water!
3. Rent a pontoon boat and explore the lake.
4. Plan a surprise picnic.
5. Make a commitment—all vacations will be to unusual places.
6. Rent a motorcycle for a day and go to the country.

Communicating Your Love

1. Hide a gift or note of love each month. The consistency of this event, and its "extreme" nature by comparison with what others would consider the norm, will make you memorable.
2. Laugh at his jokes, even when they aren't funny.
3. Listen to whatever she wants to talk about.
4. Send a telegram to your spouse at work.
5. Rent a billboard.
6. Hire a sky writer.
7. Tape a banner to the house or car.
8. Send a message in a bottle.
9. Send a thank-you gift to your spouse when you get promoted.
10. Send a barrage of cards and messages—one each day for ten consecutive days.
11. Write in his name for president in the election booth.

Using Hiding Places

1. Frequently hide notes and tokens of love. Consider these fun places to hide them:
   - Under the bed pillow
   - In his luggage, to be found when he arrives at his destination
   - In the medicine cabinet
   - In the laundry basket
   - On the end of a fishing pole
   - On the birdbath
   - On the dash of the car
   - In the console of the car
   - At the bottom of the swimming pool
   - In his tool chest
   - In a pair of socks
   - In the sleeve of a coat.
   - In her handbag

2. Or hide some small items in food, for instance,
   - Ice cubes
   - Pieces of cake
   - Bowls of Jello or pudding
   - Baked potatoes
   - Veggies

Getting Close

1. Take off your modesty in private moments.
2. Draw a bubble bath and pour a glass of bubbly!
3. Create a secret code word between the two of you that means "I love you," or "Let's get away privately for a while."
4. Write a secret message in the steam on the bathroom mirror.
5. Suntan his initials on your thigh. (They will fade in time.)
6. Arrange a spontaneous date after work for dinner and...

Saying It With Flowers, Food, and Music

1. Send a bouquet with a message in the language of flowers. (See the language of flowers at the end of this chapter.)

2. Pick a flower when passing by and present it to her.
3. Plan a private concert featuring his favorite musician.
4. Send a barber shop quartet to sing songs that convey your message.
5. Send a case of his favorite drink or a bushel of oranges.
6. Dedicate a song to her over the radio.
7. Dance in the dark.
8. Dance anywhere. No music needed. Make your own.
9. Contract with a songwriter to write a special song.
10. Inscribe a bottle of wine.
11. Contract with a vineyard to produce your own private label of wine.
12. Eat ice cream together from the gallon container.
13. Serenade her outside your bedroom window.
14. Name a wildflower after her.
15. Name something after him—a goldfish, a favorite recipe, a garden, or a tradition that you mutually create.
16. Touch hands during the family dinner prayer.
17. Quietly restate your wedding vows during the "vows" portion of weddings you attend, or repeat them on your anniversary.
18. Write a secret message on the 2 x 4 boards in your house for future generations to find and read.

Working at It

1. Hire a cleaning lady for a day so she can catch up on her chores.
2. Hire a lawn man for a day so he can catch up on his chores.
3. Wrap up a gift certificate for the household chore she least likes to do—ironing perhaps.
4. Handmake a gift.
5. Put your handprints or footprints in any new cement you pour.
6. Don't ask your spouse to do what you can do for yourself.

That's Entertainment

1. Get tickets to his favorite sports team.
2. Get tickets to her favorite TV show. Many shows offer complimentary tickets.

3. Put his name on the scoreboard at the ballpark.
4. Schedule an appointment for her with a psychic.
5. Make an appointment for him with a massage therapist.
6. Blindfold her and drive her to her favorite private location for dinner and entertainment.
7. Plan a weekend getaway as a surprise.
8. Send a limousine rather than a taxi cab.

Let the Child in You Come Out and Play

1. Go swinging together in the park.
2. Go wading in the public fountain.
3. Go fly a kite.
4. Fill her bedroom or office with inflated balloons.
5. Create a scavenger hunt in your house or office and win a gift as the end prize.

Kids' Stuff: Things to Do to Make Yourself Memorable to Your Children

Children need a lot of things, especially attention. Arnold Glasgow advised, "The best thing to spend on children is your time." Take ordinary events and make them into extraordinary events with a little creativity and free thinking. Consider the following ideas for making memorable moments with your kids:

Security Blanket

1. Always part with words of love. Always greet with words of love. Say "I love you" frequently.
2. Hold hands routinely. Start young and keep it going through teenage and adult years. A special feeling of connectedness is created when people touch. Have you hugged your child today?
3. Whenever trouble arises, be there for support and defense.
4. Pick a theme of encouragement and maintain it throughout your child's life. For example, "Champ" is a good theme for boys. It inspires excellence and the ambition to win. On as many occasions as possible, find appropriate gifts symbolizing the theme of "champ." It might be a hat

or a T-shirt that says "champ" on it. It might be a banner from the championship team of the season. Anything that symbolizes "champ" and "you're the best" will do. Be consistent with the theme throughout life. The theme could lead to a nickname.

5. Ask your children's advice on small and large questions. Incorporate as many of their ideas as possible into the final plan.

6. Select a charity that your children identify with and participate with them in supporting it. The humane society for animals is a popular one with smaller children.

7. Underpromise and overdeliver.

Body & Brain (B&B)

1. On vacations, require a morning chore consisting of both body and brain activities, such as a half hour of exercise and a half hour of reading or other mental challenge. B&B becomes a task that's done right after room pickup, a must before the zoo of activity planned for the rest of the day. Initially they may complain, but at summer's end they'll thank you.

2. Introduce them to the experience of art in life at museums, art institutes, theaters, and concerts. Children may, or may not, appreciate it at an early age or at the time of the event, but in retrospect they will look upon such experiences as memorable.

3. Go for long bicycle rides together and let the one you're with be lead pedaler.

4. Go canoeing and let your child be lead paddler.

5. Encourage any physical activity. Stronger bodies lead to improved confidence.

6. Go camping together. Anything outside is better!

7. Build a clubhouse together.

8. Camp out in the backyard overnight together.

The Gift of Communication

1. Use symbols and stories to teach lessons.

2. Learn to be a master storyteller.

3. Write a poem for your children.

4. Tape a banner to their clubhouse.
5. Write a letter to each child every year of his or her life. Put copies of the letters away in a file along with your will. On your demise they will have a lifetime of messages from you.
6. Compile a scrapbook of "life advice" from famous people.
7. Send a message in a bottle to them.
8. Laugh at their jokes even when you don't understand them or have heard them a thousand times before.
9. Learn the lyrics to their favorite song.
10. Turn the volume up and sing together in the car.
11. Nominate them for an award or honor.
12. Give a prepaid telephone calling card to a child going away to school or on a trip.
13. Make 100 wishes in the fountain by tossing 100 individual pennies in.
14. Dedicate a song to them on the radio.
15. Send them mail—cards, letters, riddles, jokes, cartoons.
16. Tell nightly stories to create pleasant dreams.
17. Create a secret sign language covering "I love you," "Go get 'em champ," "Good luck!" and so on.
18. Establish a weekly date with each child—a special day and time when you meet to do something together.
19. Make a date for daily talk time—maybe just fifteen minutes at the end of each day. Talk about anything— stars in the sky, where things come from, what's next in life, what's on their mind. Be ruthlessly protective of this date. Continue the daily date idea from early childhood through their adult years. Talk time may move from being face-to-face to being over the telephone when they go to college or move out on their own. Protect the tradition.
20. Pray together routinely. Go to church or synagogue together.

Building Family Memories

1. Build a time capsule with family photos and individual messages for those who discover the time capsule. Bury it in the backyard.

2. Keep a diary of your life for your children to read at some distant future date.
3. Make a scrapbook of their lives during the years they have lived with you.
4. Look through old photos together.
5. Bronze their baby shoes.
6. Have family photos taken routinely, and don't forget to include yourself in each one.
7. Give each child, at an appropriate age, part of the family heritage—a piece of furniture, a photograph, some jewelry, or an antique family item they find interesting or attractive.
8. Establish holiday traditions that bind you together—for example, a Christmas caroling evening you do each year or an Easter egg hunt you host each year. Carry the traditions to an extreme, beyond what might otherwise seem like an appropriate age level. Make it fun.
9. Build a history of dated Christmas ornaments for each child, starting with the birth year and continuing forever.
10. Hand down honored family traditions in a ceremonious way, demonstrating your understanding that the child is maturing.
11. Plant a garden or tree and name it after a child.
12. Plant a family forest of trees, one for each family member.
13. Make videotapes of as many family and individual events as possible. Videos grow more valuable as the years go by.
14. Create a fund-raising effort and attach your children's names to it or establish a small grant or college fund that holds the family name.
15. Create a traditional family gift that is given to each child when he or she reaches a particular age. A family signet ring or pocket watch are good examples that emotionally bind sons to the family identity. For girls, the family crest on a charm or a ring works well.
16. With older children who have moved away, share pieces of your garden, like pieces of your heart, transferring them from house to house and from generation to generation. Take cuttings and transplant them. Share the symbolism.

It's Party Time!

1. Hire a marching band for one of the children's backyard birthday parties.
2. Take the children to a water park and go on the giant slide with them.
3. Send a balloon bouquet to school for a child's birthday.
4. Hire a magician for a special event, featuring your child as the magician's assistant.
5. Get audience tickets for their favorite TV show, or the autograph of their favorite rock star.
6. Have a squirt gun fight.
7. Build a tree house together.
8. Let them bury you in the sand at the beach.
9. Take them to see their favorite hero—a ball player, an actress, a rock star.
10. Get matching outfits—father and son, or mother and daughter.
11. Dance together anytime the rhythm or mood strikes. Dance together when there is no music. Dance to the overhead music in a record store or on an elevator.
12. Take an individual vacation with each child. Do something new. Go somewhere you've not been before. Make it an adventure.
13. Adopt "your song"—one that represents a message that is special for just the two of you.

Remembering First Opportunities

1. Be the first to show them how to shave.
2. Be the first to teach them how to drive.
3. Be the first to trust them to go to the store alone.
4. Establish their first savings account with them. Make the first deposit of $100 to get it started and make it exciting.
5. Be the first to help them get the fashionable hairstyle.
6. Take them on their first airplane ride.
7. Pick out the family pet together, and let the child make the final decision.
8. Make occasional exceptions to family rules, letting them have their way on something that is really important to them.

9. Help them buy their first car, or give them the keys to the family auto for that all-important date.
10. Teach them a skill that you are particularly good at.

Staying Tight With Peers

1. Host an overnight pajama party. Boys like these as much as girls. Stay up all night with them!
2. Place the largest, most outrageous order for cookies, candy, or any other fund-raising item they are promoting.
3. Invite their friends over to your house routinely. Make your house the center of activity, the place to meet.
4. Take all their friends out for pizza and ice cream.

Being True to Your School

1. Attend the father-daughter school dance wearing an outfit just as fancy as her dress is.
2. Attend the mother-son dance. Practice the dance routine in advance so you look exceptional on the dance floor.
3. Send a pizza delivery man to school with an extra large pizza for your children's lunch.
4. Attend football practice and cheer!
5. Show up for all the teacher conferences. Let the staff know of your support for your child, and for them as professionals.
6. Fund a special classroom experience for them and their classmates.
7. Have teammates sign the team ball as a keepsake for your child.

Bylaws for In-Laws

Making yourself memorable with in-laws is not as difficult as it might initially seem. The following ideas will help create a stronger bond earlier in the relationship. Personalize each concept to meet your situation.

1. Treat in-laws with extreme respect.
2. Defer to in-laws in conversation, asking for their advice and opinions.

3. Act as a conduit to strengthen their relationships with grandchildren by telling your children interesting or heroic stories about them.
4. Take exceptional care of their daughter or son—your spouse—and let them know about the extra care you provide.
5. Make them feel like heroes.
6. Buy them a big gift—a car, an entertainment center, something extreme.
7. Send a gift to their pet.
8. Avoid discussions regarding sex, politics, or religion.
9. Put a small gift at their dinner place setting.
10. Create a tradition especially for them.
11. Give gifts of labor.
12. Give gifts of time.
13. Place a welcome note or small gift on the bed pillow when they come to visit.
14. Be generous with compliments.
15. Underpromise and overdeliver.
16. Welcome each of their initiatives to visit with you.

Memorable Image-Destroyers

To create a favorable and memorable image requires taking specific initiatives. It also calls for avoiding negative image-destroyers.

Image destroyers are actions that demolish, in one fell swoop, all the positive work done thus far. Steer clear of the following destructive behaviors in order to allow the uninterrupted growth of a positive and memorable image:

1. *Damaging accusations.* Accusations of any nature are damaging. True or false, accusations result in emotional hurt and scarring that can greatly dilute both your past and future efforts to create a favorable image. Once made, accusations, even if they have been withdrawn, always leave a residue of bad feelings. Avoid making accusations against others, steer clear of having accusations made against you, and beware of self-administered accusations and put-downs.

2. *Emotional outrages.* Yelling, screaming, and going on end-lessly about something that has angered you are common forms of emotional outrage. Although these outbursts may seem com-pletely justified in your eyes, their impact is intensely negative and may well result in creating a dominant negative memory of you or, at best, in diluting or even destroying all the positive memorable efforts that have gone before.

3. *Negative names.* Negative words are magnetic. They stick to the person you send them to. Negative name calling and epi-thets such as "stupid," "dumb," "worthless," and others are not forgotten. Using them is a destructive behavior that often has its roots in what others mistakenly think is fun. Avoid negative name calling for any person and for any reason.

4. *Random dependability.* Consistency and dependability, cousins to one another, are essential to creating a favorable image. Inconsistency and undependability of behavior fre-quently translate to a reduced level of trust in you, a lack of con-fidence that makes the creation of memorable moments more difficult. Random behavior of any nature can be the kiss of death for future memorable events you wish to create.

11

Consolation Prizes

"No age or time of life, no position or circumstance, has a monopoly on success."

—*Gerrard*

People being what they are, we can project with certainty that the concepts, strategies, and techniques for making yourself memorable will be successful in the great majority of situations, provided there is a positive, win-win opportunity to start with. The extent to which your efforts will be successful is directly correlated to the amount of time, heart, and interest you invest in a win-win effort.

Unfortunately, not all relationships lend themselves to a winning opportunity. There are circumstances that uncontrollably represent a no-win situation from the start. In these cases, no strategy to make yourself memorable will be effective. We can define the circumstances that make for win-win situations, as well as those that would project a no-win situation.

Win-Win Situations

Win-win circumstances are those in which all the parties involved benefit from the effort or experience. Indeed, it is a winning situation from every perspective.

The strategies and techniques to make yourself memorable are effective in win-win solutions when there is a certain state of readiness among participants. The state of readiness may be something the individual is consciously aware of. Or it may be a subconscious readiness, something the individual is not entirely aware of; yet it does, in fact, exist. In either case, a significant readiness factor is required in order to make yourself memorable.

The following characteristics are indicative of a level of readiness for win-win situations where the strategies and techniques for making yourself memorable will be effective. Not all characteristics on this list need to be present in order to create a memorable event. The more characteristics that are present, the stronger is the indication that the parties are ready to create and accept memorable relationships. Check your situation against this list of readiness factors:

Win-Win Readiness Factors

1. There is a mutual or complementary desire and willingness among participants to interact with one another.
2. All parties participate. Some lead and some follow, but everybody is doing something in the process.
3. There is a sense of boldness, daring, adventure, and experimentation on the part of at least one participant.
4. Personal acts of reaching out are evident from all parties.
5. There is some degree of giving from all participants.
6. Actions are geared to serve another's interest, not a self-interest.
7. Actions are growth-oriented, developmental, or helpful to all parties.

Win-win situations are self-perpetuating. The rewards and satisfactions experienced from being party to a successful relationship creates the desire to do more of the same; a cycle of winning and memorable experiences results.

No-Win Situations

No-win circumstances are those in which it is impossible to achieve success regardless of the efforts made or the resources consumed. As Thomas Fuller, the historic English chaplain to King Charles II, stated, "It's a silly game where nobody wins." In no-win situations, nobody wins.

The optimistic part of me wants to say that there is no such thing as a no-win situation. That, in fact, every situation has the potential for being a winning one. However, the face of reality proves this to be wrong. There are, indeed, situations where regardless of the effort, strategy, desire, or resources expended, attempts to create a memorable relationship, image, or event will not be successful. There are people who, regardless of your generous acts or heart-filled efforts, are not interested in or not capable of creating or being a party to a memorable event or relationship with you. There are no-win circumstances.

The following list of no-win indicators has been compiled to save you the pain and trouble of trial and error. The existence of any one indicator is generally enough to qualify the situation as no-win. The more no-win indicators present in your situation, the more certain it is that the techniques and strategies to make yourself memorable will be fruitless.

No-Win Indicators

1. There is no desire or willingness to create any level of relationship or experience by one or more of the parties.
2. Some parties participate, but others don't reciprocate.
3. There is a sense of confinement to the status quo, a fear of, or disregard for, something new by one or more of the parties.
4. Acts of withdrawal are made by one or more of the parties.
5. There is only receiving, no reciprocal giving.
6. Actions by one or more of the parties are geared to their self-interests only.
7. Actions by one or more of the parties are self-centered and self-defeating.

No-win circumstances are saddening because, inevitably, when people are unable to connect they lose something of unknown value, very possibly the opportunity to share valuable experiences and to create together wonderful memories.

Claiming the Prizes

What is the value of making yourself memorable? What is the value of reviving lost or faded relationships, of being remembered by your family and friends, of standing out in a competitive society? What is the value of being the customer magnet of your industry? The answers to these questions represent the valuable prizes that memorable people claim.

The changed behaviors and increased sensitivities learned through memory-making strategies and techniques will change you as a person. For each calculated and planned memorable event that you create, an equal number of unplanned memorable opportunities will occur, which you are now in a position to transform into additional memorable events. Soon these new behaviors will become second nature to you, a natural extension of the more memorable you.

The potential to create a memorable event or image exists in every person. When the readiness factors change, and a no-win situation takes on the characteristics of a win-win situation, the opportunity to make yourself memorable is created. It all boils down to a matter of synchronized technique and timing.

Addendum

In the language of flowers each flower has a special meaning. The meaning of some of the more popular flowers and their messages are:

Flower	Meaning
Daisy	Innocence
Daffodil	Regard and chivalry
Dandelion	Oracle
Forget-me-not	True love
Hollyhock	Female ambition
Iris	Message
Ivy	Fidelity
Lavender	Distrust
Lilac	First emotions of love
Lily	Purity
Lily of the valley	Return of happiness
Peony	Shame and bashfulness
Rose	Love
Sunflower	Haughtiness
Carnation	Alas! for my poor heart
Cornflower	Delicacy
Geranium	Melancholy
Marigold	Grief
Narcissus	Egotism
Water lily	Purity of heart

Bibliography

Auletta, Ken. *The Art of Corporate Success*. New York: G. P. Putnam's Sons, 1984.

Bennis, W. *On Becoming a Leader*. Reading, Mass.: Addison-Wesley, 1989.

Boone, Louis E. *Quotable Business*. New York: Random House, 1992.

Cohen, H. *You Can Negotiate Anything*. New York: Bantam Books, 1980.

Davidow, W. H., and B. Uttal. *Total Customer Service*. New York: HarperCollins, 1989.

Dawson, Roger. *Secrets of Power Persuasion*. Englewood Cliffs, N.J.: Prentice Hall, 1992.

Derr, C. B. *Managing the New Careerists: The Diverse Career Success Orientations of Today's Workers*. San Francisco: Jossey-Bass, 1986.

Douglass, M. E., and D. N. Douglass. *Manage Your Time, Manage Your Work, Manage Yourself*. New York: AMACOM, 1980.

Drucker, Peter F. *Innovation and Entrepreneurship*. New York: HarperBusiness, 1993. Originally published by Harper & Row, 1985.

Evans, Richard. *Richard Evans' Quote Book*. Salt Lake City: Publishers Press, 1971.

Flagg, Fannie, Gail Godwin, Moms Mabley, Amy Tan, Isak Dinesen, Edna O'Brien, Gertrude Stein, Bette Davis, and Julia Child. *The Wit and Wisdom of Women*. Philadelphia: Running Press, 1993.

Fisher, R., and W. Ury. *Getting to Yes*. New York: Penguin, 1983.

Forbes, B. C. *Thoughts on the Business of Life*. 2 vols. New York: B.C. Forbes & Sons Publishing, 1976.

Gabarro, J. J. *The Dynamics of Taking Charge*. Boston: Harvard Business School Press, 1987.

Grover, R. *The Disney Touch*. Homewood, Ill: BusinessOne Irwin, 1991.

Karlins, Marvin, and Herbert Abelson. *Persuasion*. 2nd ed. New York: Springer Publishing Company, 1970.

Liswood, L. A. *Serving Them Right*. New York: HarperCollins, 1990.

MacKay, Harvey. *Swim With the Sharks*. New York: William Morrow and Company, 1988.

McCormack, Mark H. *What They Don't Teach You at Harvard Business School*. New York: Bantam Books, 1984.

McWilliams, Peter, and John-Roger. *Do It!* Los Angeles: Prelude Press, 1991.

McWilliams, Peter, and John-Roger. *Life 101*. Los Angeles: Prelude Press, 1991.

Paul, John II. *Crossing the Threshold of Hope*. New York: Alfred A. Knopf, 1994.

Pickles, Sheila. *The Language of Flowers*. New York: Harmony Books, 1989.

Safire, William, and Leonard Safire. *Good Advice*. New York: Wings Books, 1982.

Salk, Lee. *Familyhood*. New York: Simon & Shuster, 1992.

Tannen, Deborah. *Talking From 9 to 5*. New York: Avon Books, 1995.

Wheeler, Elmer. *How to Put Yourself Across*. New York: Bramhall House, 1962.

Index